Royal Horticultural Society

RHS PRUNING & TRAINING

Royal Horticultural Society

RHS PRUNING & TRAINING

MITCHELL BEAZLEY

RHS PRUNING & TRAINING

First published in Great Britain in 2012 by Mitchell Beazley,
an imprint of Octopus Publishing Group Ltd, Endeavour House,
189 Shaftesbury Avenue, London WC2H 8JY
www.octopusbooks.co.uk

An Hachette UK Company
www.hachette.co.uk

Published in association with The Royal Horticultural Society

Design and layout copyright © Octopus Publishing Group Ltd 2012
Text copyright © The Royal Horticultural Society 2012

The publishers will be grateful for any information that will assist
them in keeping future editions up to date. Although all reasonable
care has been taken in the preparation of this book, neither the
publishers nor the authors can accept any liability for any
consequence arising from the use thereof, or the information
contained therein.

ISBN: 978 1 84533 630 1

A CIP record for this book is available from the British Library

Set in Gill Sans and Minion
Printed and bound in China

Author Geoff Hodge
Publisher Lorraine
Commissioning Ed
Senior Editor Lear
Copy-editor Joann
Proofreader Lesley
Indexer Helen Snai
Art Director Jonat
Senior Art Editor J
Designer Lizzie Ba
Picture Research M
Production Manag
RHS Commissioni

CONTENTS

• INTRODUCTION •

To many gardeners, pruning or cutting back plants can be confusing and complicated – but it does not have to be.

The purpose of pruning is to influence the way plants grow, to improve their growth and therefore their shape and flower and fruit production.

Some plants need very little pruning, while others require annual pruning to ensure a good display. Overgrown plants, which have never been pruned or have been pruned badly, may need severe pruning to restore them to their former glory.

Some gardeners worry unnecessarily that cutting off even the smallest twig will have dire consequences for the plant. In fact, most plants are very forgiving and respond well to pruning.

Some even thrive on being cut back hard. On the other hand, there are some plants that do not really like being pruned hard or at all.

PRUNING APPROACHES

There are two different approaches to pruning. Some gardeners are constantly snipping off little bits here and there, tidying up their plants to give them a neat overall appearance. Others prefer to hard prune their plants, cutting them down to ground level.

Constant tidying up and lightly tipping back plants may make the growth unbalanced, topheavy or lopsided and, if done at the wrong time of year, will also remove flower buds and therefore result in no display later on.

For best results, you need to be somewhere in the middle – hard pruning those plants that need it

Hard pruning or even renovation pruning is often needed by plants.

Most plants respond well to accurate pruning above a bud or pair of buds.

6

BUD TYPES

Apical or terminal bud
This appears at the tip of a stem and controls its length and growth pattern. If the apical bud is removed or damaged, it allows buds lower down to shoot.

Lateral buds
These are usually formed at the nodes – where a leaf joins a stem. They will develop into leaves or sideshoots, usually in their first year.

Dormant buds
A lateral bud that for some reason does not continue developing. Pruning a nearby apical bud is likely to stimulate it into growth, producing new leaves or stems.

Adventitious buds
These are formed only when required, after damage or pruning has occurred and there are no dormant buds nearby. They produce new leaves or stems, and are often the buds that come into growth when hard, renovation pruning has been carried out.

In some trees, several buds break at the same point, producing a profusion of thin stems called water shoots (see p68).

Vegetative and fruit buds
Vegetative buds are usually small and thin and go on to produce leaves. Fruit buds are fatter and contain the embryo flowers. By pruning it is possible to change vegetative buds into fruiting buds, which is why fruit pruning is so important.

and just lightly cutting back plants that respond better to such an approach. Plants of the latter group generally do not reshoot from old wood.

Pruning is not always the answer to reducing the size of a plant, because the harder and the more often you prune a plant, the stronger it will regrow. So, once you start pruning, you may have to continue to do it regularly.

HOW PLANTS GROW
In order to prune correctly it helps to understand how plants grow and how they respond to pruning.

New extension growth is usually made just below the apical or terminal bud. This bud dominates the other buds; that is, while it is still in place it inhibits the growth of buds below it and on lateral growth or sideshoots. When it is removed, the dominance is lost and buds lower down start to shoot. So, cutting back a stem or removing its tip triggers buds below it to develop and results in bushier growth.

In some plants, a single sideshoot may grow away strongly and reinstate the apical dominance; in others, two or more growing points share the dominance and produce dual or multiple leaders. In trees, this can lead to problems later on, so the weakest leader or leaders should be removed to retain the strongest and/or straightest stem.

Pulling down a vertical shoot and training it horizontally can also break apical dominance. Sideshoots are produced along the shoot and these are much more likely to flower and fruit. This technique is particularly useful when training climbers, wall shrubs and several trained fruit shapes.

Removing large branches may be necessary when reshaping a tree.

BUYING PLANTS

Although it is possible to correct poor growth by pruning, it is far better to start with well-shaped, good-quality plants in the first place. This will ensure you get the best out of your plants, and that they produce the displays you are after.

When buying, you should therefore select bushy, well-balanced plants. Top growth should be strong and healthy, with no signs of pest damage. Remove each plant from its container and check that the roots are not pot-bound, that is growing in dense circles.

RULES & TOOLS

• INTRODUCTION •

Whenever you prune, there must be a good reason to do so. This sounds obvious, but some people prune just for the sake of it or because they are not sure what to do. The main reasons for pruning are:

● To improve initial shape and early training by formative pruning.

● To create or maintain the required shape and habit.

● To restrict a plant to the required height and/or width.

● To remove weak, crossing, rubbing and overcrowded growth.

● To remove dead, diseased, dying or damaged growth – the 4Ds.

● To improve flowering.

● To improve fruiting.

● To improve foliage and stem growth and/or shape and/or colour.

● To shape a plant decoratively.

● To remove reverted growth, unwanted suckers and other unwanted stems.

Remember these reasons before and during tackling any pruning jobs – they will help you decide which parts of the plant need removing. And remember that if a plant is one that needs pruning, it is far better to carry this out regularly when needed

Correct pruning can improve the overall shape, height and flowering potential of many plants.

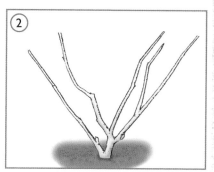

After planting, for the first few years remove stems that are crowded or crossing, as these will spoil the symmetry of the plant. This is especially important for trees and shrubs that do not like hard pruning when they are older, such as magnolia and witch hazel (Hamamelis).

Prune so the plant has evenly spaced branches and a balanced, open habit. This forms the permanent woody framework from which the rest of the plant develops. As the plant continues to grow, aim to maintain this open habit on the new growth.

rather than leaving it until more major renovation surgery becomes necessary.

On a large tree or shrub, it can be difficult to know where to start. Always begin by: removing the 4Ds (see page 16); then cutting out weak, crossing, rubbing, overcrowded and reverted growth; then suckers (see p69); and, finally, pruning to maintain, size, shape and habit and to improve the required attribute (flowers, fruit, foliage or stems).

FORMATIVE PRUNING

Many trees and shrubs naturally develop a well-shaped structure without any help. Others benefit in the first year or so from formative pruning, especially if they need only minimal pruning when mature.

Young trees, particularly whips and feathered whips (see pp25 and 27), need formative pruning to build up a good branch structure. Similarly, young fruit trees and most fruit bushes benefit from formative pruning. Shrubs and trees, especially fruit trees, grown in a restricted form – such as cordons, espaliers and fans (see p129) – require careful pruning in the first couple of years so that they build up the desired shape.

Formative pruning of shrubs that are pruned hard annually is not so important. However, it does helps to encourage a balanced shape with well-spaced branches.

For more details, see the chapters dealing with these subjects.

MAINTAINING PLANT SHAPE & HABIT

Although many plants look more natural when left to their own devices, there are many that thrive on being pruned to provide a certain effect or shape. And the reverse is also true – some plants, especially rampant climbers, look much better if they are strictly trained and pruned; left to grow unchecked they soon become tangled.

Even natural-looking plants can produce growth that spoils their look, shape or symmetry or becomes dangerous, and this needs removing. Some trees, for example, may produce low branches that do not allow access for mowing under or could cause an accident if someone walked into them by mistake.

If one side of the plant grows more vigorously than the other, leading to a lopsided shape, you can lightly prune the stronger-growing shoots and hard prune the weaker ones to restore the balance of the plant.

PRUNING AN ESTABLISHED PLANT

CORRECT PRUNING CUTS
To even out the growth of a lopsided shrub, cut back the overlong growth lightly, but hard prune weaker growth.

SHRUB AFTER CORRECT PRUNING
Pruning this way will ensure the shrub produces much more even growth.

INCORRECT PRUNING CUTS
You should not hard prune the overlong growth or prune the whole plant evenly all over.

SHRUB AFTER INCORRECT PRUNING
Pruning this way will make the shrub grow even more lopsided.

PRUNING TO SIZE

This is often the commonest reason for pruning, and is usually because a plant has been grown in the wrong place.

If the plant has grown far too large for its space and hard pruning is necessary, such severe cutting back may prevent it from performing correctly for a year or two; it may also seriously weaken the plant or even kill it. A plant that is cut back several times a year will become unbalanced, topheavy, and often flowerless.

On the other hand, there are many plants that thrive on hard pruning, producing vigorous regrowth that will flower the same year – these are perfect choices for limited spaces. And there are numerous dwarf cultivars of many popular, taller-growing plants that may be better choices for small areas.

Where a plant is constantly being cut back because it is growing too tall or wide for its space and, as a result, the display is spoilt, it may be better to remove it altogether and replace with something more suitable.

REMOVING UNWANTED GROWTH

Often, pruning can be limited to just removing unwanted growth, such as weak, crossing, rubbing or overcrowded stems on a plant.

Some plants naturally produce a mass of weak, thin growth that spoils their shape, while others do so as a result of being incorrectly pruned. Such weak growth is unlikely to perform well and, if produced in the centre of the plant, can lead to pest and disease build-up, as well as being more prone to die-back. If allowed to develop, weak stems can also be prone to wind damage. Such growth is likely to become misshapen, too.

It may be necessary to thin out weak and spindly

When pruning, always hold the plant carefully and use sharp tools.

growth to open up the centre of a plant, allowing in more air and light, which in turn will help ripen the stems and consequently lead to more flowers and, where appropriate, fruit.

Where there is excessive growth, two or more branches may cross each other and start rubbing together, thereby causing damage to one or both of them. The weaker/weakest branch should be removed to prevent this.

Sometimes, branches arising from one side of the plant will grow into the centre of the plant and across to the other side. Crossing growth is unnecessary as it fills in the middle of the plant and can be more prone to rubbing against other branches. It should be cut out.

Remove congested growth to open up the plant and help reduce diseases.

REMOVING DEAD, DISEASED, DYING OR DAMAGED GROWTH

Any plant part that is affected by the 4Ds – as dead, diseased, dying or damaged growth is popularly known – should be cut back far enough to remove all the damage and into sound, healthy growth.

Dead growth should always be completely cut out – it serves no use to the plant and is a source of infection for the rest of the stems. Anything that is damaged, diseased or starting to die back should also be removed: for example, growth damaged by frost or by strong or cold winds.

As more and more people are looking to garden organically and fewer chemicals are available for gardeners who want to cure problems, pruning out growth that is affected by disease or badly infested by pests is a good way of controlling the problem; indeed, it is sometimes the only way.

Pests that can be wholly or partially controlled by pruning include: aphids (especially woolly aphids), red spider mite, stem-boring caterpillars and scale insects. Diseases that can be tackled in this way include: brown rot, canker, coral spot, fire blight, mildew, rust and silver leaf.

If diseased or damaged growth has already healed naturally by itself, then

Prune Caryopteris × clandonensis *annually to remove its twiggy growth.*

Cut it back hard to leave a low framework of healthy, main stems.

it is usually better to leave this in place rather than trying to cut it out, back to healthy growth.

Branches that are partially broken, such as by strong winds, grazing animals or lightning strikes, rarely mend if tied back in position and it is usually better to cut them out or shorten them to a suitable replacement stem. Damaged or torn bark, too, is most unlikely to reunite with the rest of the tree.

IMPROVING FLOWERING

Many plants will produce more flowers if they are pruned correctly, because pruning encourages plants to divert their energy into flowering growth and flower production.

Some plants will also develop bigger, better flowers if pruned regularly: pruned buddlejas, for example, produce flower spikes up to three times longer than unpruned plants.

Cutting back plants such as lilacs, roses and clematis also ensures their flowers are produced at a height that can be appreciated, rather than towering above your head.

When pruning to improve flowering it is essential to know when the plant

Well-pruned fruit trees and bushes will produce regular, healthy and bumper crops.

flowers and on what type of growth the flower buds and therefore the flowers are produced.

Generally, trees, shrubs and climbers that flower from late autumn through spring and into early summer produce their flowers or flower buds on growth formed that year (in the case of late autumn- and early winter-flowering plants) or the previous year (in mid- to late winter and spring flowerers). They are pruned immediately after flowering.

Plants that flower from midsummer into autumn do so on the current year's growth, and are pruned in early spring, usually just before or just after growth begins.

Naturally, there are some exceptions, so always check the plant in the pruning directory (see p162).

IMPROVING FRUITING

As flowers produce fruit, it follows that pruning to improve flowering will also enhance fruiting. Although you can follow this general principle for ornamental fruit and berries, pruning for edible fruit is different and usually needs more disciplined techniques. You can find out exactly how in the chapter on fruit (see p126).

IMPROVING FOLIAGE & STEM COLOUR

Many plants are grown principally for their ornamental, colourful foliage and a few for their attractive stems. Regular pruning of these plants will improve their performance.

Pruning back plants that have become bare in the middle will encourage compact, more vigorous growth with a more even covering of leaves.

Many deciduous plants grown for their foliage will produce bigger, more colourful leaves if pruned hard annually or every other year; good examples include catalpa, smoke bush (*Cotinus*), paulownia and elder (*Sambucus*). Hard pruning of evergreens rarely affects the size or colour intensity of the foliage.

Some dogwood (*Cornus*), rubus and willow (*Salix*) species are grown for their colourful winter stems. The colour intensity fades as the stems get older, so annual pruning in spring ensures plenty of fresh, new growth that will colour up well the following winter (see p44).

DECORATIVE PRUNING

Yet another reason to prune is to transform certain plants into beautiful, architectural and ornamental shapes and so create living 'sculptures'. Although topiary is the pinnacle of this art, many plants can be pruned and trained to produce specific shapes, such as 'clouds' or 'balls' (see p52).

Hard prune dogwoods (Cornus) each year to improve their stem colour.

OTHER REASONS TO PRUNE

Pruning out stems with all-green leaves on variegated plants (see p69) is also important, as is removing suckers (see p68) and even root pruning (see p74).

Decorative pruning is a great way of providing ornamentation in a garden.

Pruning cuts should always be made so that the wound heals quickly to prevent disease entering and damaging or killing the plant. Using clean, sharp cutting tools is important, as is making the right cut in the right place at the right time.

Correct timing is essential to ensure maximum flowering and fruiting (see Improving flowering, p17, and Improving fruiting, p18). However, other factors may also affect timing.

If some evergreens and slightly tender plants are pruned too early in spring, or too late in autumn, the resulting cuts or new growth may be susceptible to frost or cold wind damage. Some plants may bleed sap, which will weaken them if pruned at the wrong time. And some may be more susceptible to disease if pruning is carried out at an inappropriate season.

Before pruning, therefore, check in the plant directory (see p162) for the individual timings and requirements of your plants.

PRUNING CUTS

Always 'look twice and prune once', checking on where you should be pruning first and then make the correct cut. Whenever and whatever you prune,

the pruned growth must end in a healthy sideshoot or strong bud, whenever buds are visible. The pruning cut should be clean with no ragged edges and be as near to the bud as possible, but not so close that it damages the bud.

Never leave any growth beyond a bud or sideshoot, as it will die back. Such a 'snag' may become a source of disease infection, which may travel back through the rest of the stem.

Growth buds develop into shoots that point in the same direction as the bud. Therefore, pruning to an inward-facing bud will result in a shoot that

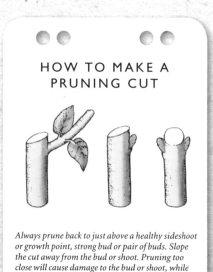

HOW TO MAKE A PRUNING CUT

Always prune back to just above a healthy sideshoot or growth point, strong bud or pair of buds. Slope the cut away from the bud or shoot. Pruning too close will cause damage to the bud or shoot, while cutting too far away will result in dieback.

grows inwards and may cause problems later if it rubs against other shoots, or produces thick growth that encourage disease problems. Outward-facing buds develop into shoots that grow away from the plant, but this may result in the plant growing too wide. So always think carefully when choosing which bud to prune back to.

The harder you prune a stem the more vigorous its regrowth, so cut back thin, weaker shoots harder than strong ones. The latter may need only light pruning or tipping back.

AFTERCARE

After pruning a plant, it is a good idea to give it a good feed with a fertiliser.

Use the right tools at the right time to ensure successful pruning results.

Liquid feeds provide a quick boost, but are short-lived; granular feeds last longer; and controlled-release fertilisers are effective for several months. Most flowering trees, shrubs and climbers respond well to feeding with a high-potash granular feed.

A plant's feeder roots are roughly distributed at the edge of the branch canopy, so spread the fertiliser in a circle in this area.

After feeding, water the soil and add a thick mulch of organic matter, such as well-rotted manure, garden compost or composted bark.

You will need a basic pruning tool kit.

SECATEURS

Bypass secateurs cut with a scissor action, although only one blade has a cutting edge. They give the cleanest cuts. Anvil secateurs have a metal plate or anvil that supports the plant stem while the blade cuts through it. They are often best used to cut dead wood. If you have weak wrists and find using secateurs difficult, try ratchet secateurs. These cut in stages and need very little pressure.

SAWS

Pruning saws are perfect for cutting through thicker wood. They have wide-set teeth that make cuts wider than the thickness of the blade, thereby reducing the risk of jamming. They may have smaller teeth at the tip of the blade to help get the cut started.

A bow saw may be the better choice where very thick branches are to be pruned, especially if they are dead.

TREE PRUNERS

These are perfect for cutting high branches where using a ladder is unsuitable or inadvisable. The cutting action on tree pruners is activated either by a lever at the bottom of the pole or via a pulley and cord system.

PRUNING KNIVES

Knives are useful for cutting back or tipping soft growth, for removing rotting and diseased material from branches and for paring the bark smooth after removing larger branches.

LOPPERS

Loppers have a wider mouth than secateurs so they can cut thicker stems. Their longer handles, and the fact that they are used two-handed, provide extra leverage, so more force can be exerted to cut thick wood.

SHEARS

Hand shears are the perfect choice for short hedges and can also be used on small-leaved plants where accurate pruning with secateurs is not necessary.

Single-handed shears and sheep-shearing shears are also available, but they are suitable only for thin, leafy growth as you cannot exert much force.

HEDGETRIMMERS

Powered hedgetrimmers are better than shears for cutting large hedges. They can be powered by electricity, petrol or rechargeable batteries, and they come in various blade lengths. Both factors affect not only how powerful they are and how quickly they will cut the hedge, but also how heavy they are. One-handed powered shrub pruners are available for trimming small-leaved plants and for topiary work.

CHAINSAWS

Chainsaws can be dangerous in the hands of inexperienced and untrained users. Generally, they are best left in the hands of a trained expert, so call in a tree surgeon for big pruning jobs.

CARING FOR YOUR TOOLS

All pruning equipment should have sharp blades, so invest in an oil or carborundum stone or a diamond sharpener and use it regularly.

After every pruning session, clean and sharpen each blade, using an emery cloth, emery paper or similar to remove caked-on plant material and sap. Clean the blades with a suitable disinfectant to avoid spreading disease from plant to plant; then wipe the blade with an oily cloth to prevent rust. Regularly, lubricate all moving parts with general household oil.

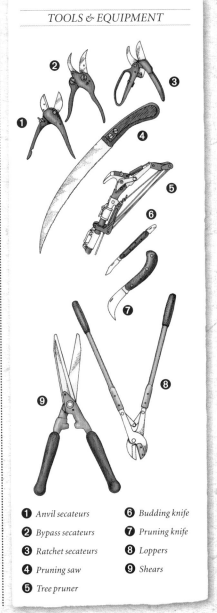

TOOLS & EQUIPMENT

❶ Anvil secateurs

❷ Bypass secateurs

❸ Ratchet secateurs

❹ Pruning saw

❺ Tree pruner

❻ Budding knife

❼ Pruning knife

❽ Loppers

❾ Shears

· UNDERSTANDING PRUNING TERMS ·

Adventitious bud see p8.

Alternate Used to describe buds, stems or leaves alternating at different levels on opposite sides of the stem.

Apex The tip of a stem.

Apical bud see p8.

Apical dominance The controlling influence of an apical bud over the growth of buds and shoots below.

Axil The place where a leaf joins a stem.

Basal shoots Shoots arising at or near ground level.

Bleeding The oozing of sap from a cut or wound.

Branch collar The thickened ring at the base of a branch.

Branch leader The leading shoot of a branch.

Branch-headed standard Tree with a clear trunk and a branched head or crown.

Breastwood The shoots that grow forward from a tree or shrub trained against a supporting structure.

Bud A condensed shoot containing an embryonic leaf, leaf cluster, flower or flowers.

Bud break The process of a leaf, shoot or flower emerging from a bud.

Callus The protective tissue formed by a plant covering a wound or wounded surface.

Cambium The layer of actively dividing cells beneath the bark on a tree. The cambium layer is the green growth layer just next to the bark.

Central leader The main central stem of a plant.

Central-leader standard A tree or shrub with a clear stem that continues as the *central leader* through the *crown* of branches.

Coppicing The process of regular pruning of a tree or shrub at or close

Axil

Breastwood

to ground level to stimulate the growth of new shoots; also known as stooling.

Cordon A plant trained to produce one main stem clothed in many short growths.

Crotch The angle between two branches or between a branch and a tree trunk.

Crown The head or branched part of a tree or standard shrub above the trunk or main stem.

Deadheading The process of removing spent flowers or flowerheads and the developing seedhead.

Deciduous Used to describe a plant that drops its leaves in autumn or winter.

Disbudding The process of removing surplus buds to help promote better flowers or fruit, or the removal of *dormant buds*.

Dormant bud see p8.

Epicormic shoot A shoot that develops from latent or *adventitious buds* under the bark.

Espalier A plant trained to have a vertical central stem and tiers of branches growing horizontally on either side.

Evergreen Used to describe a plant that retains its foliage all year.

Extension growth The new growth made to lengthen a branch or stem.

Eye A growth bud, especially of roses and grapevines.

Fan A plant trained to have its main branches radiating in a fan shape from a short trunk.

Fastigiate Used to describe a plant with branches growing vertically and almost parallel with the main stem to produce a thin, upright plant.

Feathered whip A one-year-old tree that has produced lateral shoots (known as feathers).

Framework The permanent structure of branches of a tree, shrub or climber.

Graft union The point at which a cultivar (the *scion*) is grafted onto a *rootstock*.

Growing point The top bud of a shoot.

Growth bud A bud that develops into leaves or a shoot.

Coppicing

Disbudding

Internode The length of stem between two nodes.

Lateral The side growth that appears from any shoot or root.

Lateral bud see p8.

Leader/leading shoot The main, usually central, upright, shoot on a plant.

Leg The short, clear length of stem before branching occurs on a plant.

Maiden A tree in its first year.

Maiden whip A one-year-old tree that has not developed lateral branches (see *Feathered maiden* and *Whip*).

Mulch A layer of material added to the soil surface to suppress weeds, conserve soil moisture and maintain an even soil temperature.

Multistemmed Used to describe a tree or shrub with several main stems, either arising directly from the soil or from a short main stem or leg.

Node The point on a stem where the leaves, shoots or flowers arise.

Opposite buds The buds at the same level on opposite sides of a stem.

Paring Trimming with a pruning knife.

Pinch pruning A method of pruning where soft shoot tips are removed, usually by thumb and forefinger.

Pinching back/pinching out The process of removing soft growth tips to encourage bushy growth.

Pleaching A technique where branches from a row of trees are woven together and trained to form a narrow screen or canopy.

Pollard A tree that is cut back at regular intervals to the head of the main trunk.

Pyramid A plant trained to have each tier of branches shorter than those of the tier below.

Regulated pruning The occasional removal of branches or pieces of branches to prevent congestion and stimulate younger growth.

Renewal pruning The regular removal of older growth.

Renovation pruning The hard cutting back of an old plant, often to ground level, to stimulate new growth.

Eye

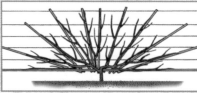

Fan

Replacement shoot A strong, young shoot that is trained or retained to replace older growth removed by pruning.

Rib The main branch of a fan-trained tree.

Rootstock The plant used to provide the roots for a grafted plant.

Scion The plant, usually a variety, that is grafted onto the *rootstock* of another plant.

Secondary growth The growth that appears after pruning.

Semievergreen Used to describe a plant that may retain its leaves in winter depending on the severity of the weather.

Sideshoot A shoot growing out from a stem.

Snag An overlong stub left behind after incorrect pruning.

Spur A small shoot or short branch bearing flowers or fruit.

Spur bearing Used to describe a plant that produces its flowers and fruit on short shoots along the stem (see *Tip bearing*).

Spur pruning The shortening of shoots to produce spurs to stimulate flower bud or fruit bud production.

Spur system The clusters of spurs produced by *spur pruning*.

Standard A tree or shrub with a clear stem below a head of branches.

Stool A plant with several shoots appearing from its base, often as a result of pruning.

Stooling see *Coppicing*.

Sublateral A sideshoot on a lateral shoot.

Tip bearing Used to describe a plant that produces its flowers and fruit at or near the shoot tips (see *Spur bearing*).

Tip pruning The process of *pinching out* or cutting back the growing tip of a shoot to remove damaged growth and/or encourage *sideshoots*.

Vegetative growth Used to describe growth that is non-flowering and usually leafy.

Whip A young tree, consisting of a single stem that has not developed lateral branches (see *Maiden whip*).

Node

Pinching back

PERENNIALS

• INTRODUCTION •

A plant flowers for one reason – to reproduce using its seeds. Once seed has been set, its work is done, so it stops flowering and concentrates its energy and reserves into ensuring the seed ripens and is distributed.

DEADHEADING

To interupt this natural process, plants can be deadheaded. Although removing the dead flowers from all plants can prove worthwhile, for well-established, trees, large shrubs and climbers this may not be feasible. However, it is usually a good idea to deadhead all new plantings to ensure they concentrate their energy on establishing properly.

Plants that have the potential to flower over a long period – such as annuals, bedding and patio perennials, herbaceous perennials and roses – respond well to deadheading, which will extend the display. Indeed, not deadheading will reduce the full potential of the display.

Because annual and herbaceous perennial stems are soft, deadheading can be done with thumb and forefinger. For thicker and woodier stems, cut with a knife, scissors, flower snips or secateurs. Always cut to a bud, sideshoot or growth point. Some low-growing herbaceous perennials, such as lady's mantle (*Alchemilla*) and cranesbill (*Geranium*), can be trimmed over with shears, removing flowering growth and old and damaged foliage. For plants such as pelargonium that produce their

WAYS IN WHICH TO DEADHEAD A STEM

For plants such as delphiniums and lupins, cut down the entire flowering stem to ground level to encourage further flowers. For plants, such as phlox, cut back to a lower set of healthy leaves.

Remove the faded flowers of bulbs along with any swelling seedpod. Bulbous plants benefit from deadheading because they can then concentrate their energy into storing food for the following year's display.

flowers on top of long stems, remove the flowering stems where they join the main stem.

After deadheading, some hardy perennials may not flower again that year, while others, especially those that start flowering early in the season, such as astrantia, delphinium, pinks (*Dianthus*), cranesbill, lupins and phlox, should reward you with further flushes of flowers.

To ensure your plants flower for as long as possible, keep them well fed with a constant supply of nutrients, especially potash.

Deadheading will ensure plants put all their energy into producing further flower buds and better-quality displays.

Some perennials, such as grasses, Chinese lantern (*Physalis*), cornflower (*Centaurea*), globe thistle (*Echinops*), golden rod (*Solidago*), honesty (*Lunaria*), *Iris foetidissima*, Michaelmas daisy (*Aster*), sedum, sunflower (*Helianthus*) and yarrow (*Achillea*), produce ornamental seedheads or fruit. All or some of these can be kept in place to enhance the garden during autumn and winter.

STOPPING

This technique is suitable for creating shorter, bushier, more sturdy plants. Stopping is particularly useful with tall perennials, such as eupatorium, helenium and veronicastrum, because it makes their stems less prone to collapsing when not artifically supported by a stake.

Cut back growth in spring by up to one third. This can be done by removing individual soft tips with finger and thumb (pinch pruning) or by cutting stems with secateurs or shears.

Pinch pruning is particularly useful on bedding and half-hardy perennials, such as argyranthemum, chrysanthemum, coleus (*Solenostemon*), fuchsia and pelargonium. It can also be used to remove flowering shoots from plants that are grown mainly for their attractive foliage; once they come into flower the quality of the foliage may be reduced.

Constantly pinching back flowering plants may delay flowering.

THINNING

Thinning is a useful method of improving the flowering display of perennials that produce a lot of multistemmed growth. It will produce stronger plants with larger flowers. Thinning out the new growth involves removing up to one in three stems at ground level when they are large enough to handle or between 10–15cm (4–6in) in height. Thinning is effective because the resulting fewer shoots have a greater share of the nutrients supplied by the root system of each plant.

PINCH PRUNING *THINNING GROWTH*

To stop plants, pinch out the growing point of each stem when it is roughly one third of its final height.

Pinch out the young shoots of multistemmed, bushy perennials, such as helenium and phlox, at their base.

THE CHELSEA CHOP

This innovative method of pruning perennials is a different type of deadheading – one that occurs before the plant actually starts to flower. It promotes later and longer flowering and keeps tall perennials more compact and less liable to collapse. It is called the Chelsea chop because the best time to do it is during or just after the RHS Chelsea Flower Show, which is held in late spring each year.

The Chelsea chop can be used on a number of mid- to late-flowering perennials, such as anthemis, aster, some bellflowers (*Campanula*), tickseed (*Coreopsis*), coneflower (*Echinacea*), helenium, sunflower, plume poppy (*Macleaya*), bergamot (*Monarda*), phlox, coneflower (*Rudbeckia*) and sedum. It is a technique that is definitely worth experimenting with.

There are several ways of tackling the Chelsea chop, depending on which plants you are cutting back and the effect you want to create.

The simplest methods are: to cut back all growth; prune every other plant; or shorten just one stem in three. Another approach is to cut back some flowering stems by a quarter, some by a half and others by up to three quarters, which results in layers of flowers at different heights and at different times.

If this sounds too drastic, you can achieve similar results with some perennials by regularly pinching out the growing tips before they flower. However, the nearer to flowering you do this, the later the plant will actually flower.

USING THE CHELSEA CHOP

In early summer, cut the plant back with shears to encourage later flowering and a shorter, more compact habit.

If using shears sounds too drastic, pinch out shoots in early summer to encourage bushy growth and later flowers.

· STAKING ·

Tall perennials and those with large flowerheads, such as peonies and dahlias, require staking, especially when grown in windy or exposed gardens or in nutrient-rich soils.

For successful staking, it is important to put the supports in place early, that is, before the plant has reached 10–15cm (4–6in) high. This not only ensures that the stems are well supported but also that the supports are hidden later on by the plant's leafy growth.

Plants with upright flower spikes, such as delphiniums and lupins, are best supported by individual stakes, such as bamboo canes, for each flower stem.

Other plants can be held up with twiggy branches, such as hazel or birch, woven willow supports, metal linking stakes or hoops.

METHODS OF STAKING PERENNIALS

Tie individual stems to a bamboo cane or similar support, with soft twine in a figure of eight. Using more than one tie will prevent the stem breaking.

Metal support hoops are sturdy and will last for years, especially if plastic coated. Most types can be lifted or extended as the plants grow through them.

Natural woven supports look attractive and are the best choice where the open nature of a plant does not produce dense enough growth to hide the support.

Metal linking and other stakes are very versatile as they can be joined in a variety of patterns and extended to support a wide range of plants.

• AUTUMN CUTBACK •

Many herbaceous perennials will start to look untidy in autumn as the plants become dormant and the current year's growth starts to die back to ground level. If this foliage is left in place, it not only looks untidy but it is also a hiding place for pests, such as slugs, and can be a site in which diseases can overwinter.

However, the old flower stems and seedheads of some perennials, including sea holly (*Eryngium*) and sedum, can provide some architectural structure to the garden over winter and these can be left in place until spring.

Tender or half-hardy perennials, such as agapanthus and red hot poker (*Kniphofia*), are best left until spring. The old foliage may protect the sensitive crown over winter.

After flowering, sedum seedheads will provide structure in the garden.

Obviously, evergreens such as bergenia, hellebore and heuchera keep most of their foliage over winter. But even these will have some of their oldest leaves looking untidy, diseased or dying and these should be removed, too.

PRUNING TASKS IN AUTUMN

In autumn or early winter, cut back or remove the old growth of deciduous perennials and tidy up around the crowns of each plant.

Not all stems add architectural form or last well through winter, and these should be removed when they start to die down.

PERENNIALS

ORNAMENTAL
SHRUBS

• INTRODUCTION •

Not all shrubs need regular or annual pruning, apart from the removal of unwanted growth and dead, dying, damaged or diseased stems. In fact, some prefer not to be pruned at all. Others benefit from cutting back every year or every other year.

The aim of regularly pruning shrubs is always to remove the oldest, less productive growth in order to provide room for younger shoots. These will perform better and help promote new growth to ensure the plant is good-looking, healthy and producing its optimum display of flowers, fruit or ornamental leaves.

Many plants that do not need regular pruning can be left for up to five years to allow a more natural look to develop. After that, they are hard pruned to around 15cm (6in) from the ground (see p42). Plants treated to severe pruning may take a couple of years to recover and flower properly again.

PRUNING DEUTZIA

FIRST YEAR
After planting in autumn or early spring, remove all thin and weak growth and cut back the tips of main stems to strong growth buds. The aim is to create a balanced, open framework.

SUBSEQUENT YEARS
Allow the plant to flower and develop strong, new stems and branches in the first growing season. Such stems and branches will become the renewal growth.

Once the flowers fade, cut back all the flowering stems to strong side branches lower down the stem. Prune thinner branches harder than thicker ones. Cut out weak and misplaced stems.

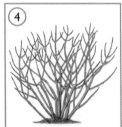

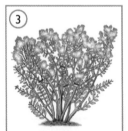

By winter, strong side branches will have grown to replace the old flowering stems. This is the renewal growth that will flower in the coming year and is similarly pruned after flowering.

• PRUNING DECIDUOUS SHRUBS •

Shrubs that flower on stems produced the previous year are pruned after flowering to encourage young and vigorous shoots that will flower in subsequent years. This method of pruning annually is often referred to as renewal pruning.

Such pruning also prevents the plants outgrowing their space and ensures flowers are produced in abundance lower down on the plant. Stems that have flowered are cut back to strong, new shoots after flowering. The resulting growth flowers the following year.

Renewal pruning can be used for most winter-, spring- and early summer flowering shrubs: for example, deutzia (see left), mock orange (*Philadelphus*) and weigela. It should be carried out every, or every other, year.

A few deciduous shrubs, such as kerria (see below), that produce almost all of their new growth from or close to ground level, need a slightly different pruning technique. Their flowered stems are cut right back to the base, or to a growth point or bud low down on stems that have vigorous, new growth.

PRUNING KERRIA

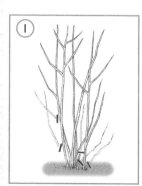

FIRST YEAR
After planting, cut back all thin and weak growth to a strong bud or growth point to create a balanced framework of branches.

After flowering, remove all flowered stems at their base or low down on the stem where new growth is forming. Mulch around the base of the plant, if necessary.

SUBSEQUENT YEARS
Prune annually after flowering, as in step 2. The new stems that form and grow will flower the following year.

• MINIMAL DECIDUOUS PRUNING •

Numerous deciduous shrubs develop a permanent framework of branches and require very little pruning once they have become established. These include magnolia, smoke bush (*Cotinus*), euonymus and witch hazel (*Hamamelis*).

Many of these naturally produce growth and flowers from the perimeter of their permanent branch framework, rather than lots of vigorous, new growth from the base of the plant and lower branches. They therefore need early training and pruning in order to build up a basic framework that will support an attractive and well-balanced branch structure.

In subsequent years, only minimal pruning is needed, in order to remove dead, diseased or damaged branches and to cut out wayward branches that are in the way or spoiling the structure and symmetry. Vigorous, new stems can either be removed if not needed or trained to replace very old branches.

PRUNING DECIDUOUS MAGNOLIA

FIRST YEAR
After planting, from autumn to early spring, remove weak growth and crossing branches to create an open, balanced framework of stems.

SECOND YEAR
In spring, preferably after flowering, remove any badly spaced side branches. Leave all other branches unpruned.

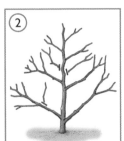

THIRD & SUBSEQUENT YEARS
Keep pruning to a minimum, removing in spring only dead, dying, diseased or damaged branches or those that are crossing.

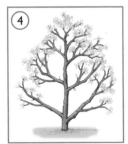

New growth and flowers emerge at the perimeter of the framework. Any further pruning should be minimal and carried out after flowering.

Japanese maples need minimal pruning once the branch framework has been created.

HYDRANGEAS

Although flowering in late summer, mophead and lacecap hydrangeas produce their flowers from buds high on the stems, developed the previous year.

Once a basic framework has been created by formative pruning (see p13), only minimal pruning is needed thereafter on established hydrangeas,

especially mopheads. This should also be delayed until mid- to late spring as the old flowerheads left on the plant can provide frost protection to the flower buds below. Harder pruning will remove the flower buds.

If old plants have become congested with lots of thin growth, carry out renewal pruning (see p39). However, as such a remedy is likely to prevent flowering that year, it is better to prune one third of the plant each year over a three-year period. At least, this ensures some flowers each year.

PRUNING HYDRANGEA

In spring, cut back the flowering stems to a pair of strong buds high on the stem. On congested plants, prune back to their base up to one third of the oldest and thinnest branches to produce renewal growth.

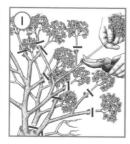

By late summer, the upper growth buds on the pruned shoots will have grown and the strongest will have produced flowerheads. New basal shoots will have developed but will not flower until the following year.

• HARD DECIDUOUS PRUNING •

Shrubs that flower on growth produced during spring and summer of the current year can be hard pruned at a suitable time in spring. This hard pruning will produce vigorous, new stems that will flower later that year.

Shrubs that can be pruned in this way are mostly those that flower in summer (especially late summer) and autumn.

It is often a good idea to wait until growth buds start to shoot before pruning, although the exact timing for the hard pruning can depend on when new growth starts to be produced and on the hardiness of the plant. Shrubs that are on the borderline of hardiness, such as fuchsia and phygelius, can be damaged by frost if pruned too early and are best left until midspring – or later if severe cold weather is a possibility.

There are several different ways of hard pruning deciduous shrubs.

Those that do not form a permanent framework of branches, such as fuchsia and Himalayan honeysuckle (*Leycesteria*), can be pruned down to or just above ground level.

Hard pruning will encourage strong, new growth and a good floral display.

PRUNING BUDDLEJA

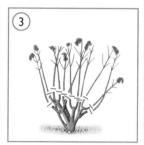

FIRST YEAR
Completely remove any weak and thin stems. Cut back all other shoots by up to two thirds to strong growth buds, emerging shoots or growth points.

Vigorous, new stems develop and flower at their tips in summer. These can be deadheaded after flowering to conserve energy and prevent seeding.

SECOND YEAR
In spring, cut back all shoots to within one or two pairs of buds on the previous year's growth.

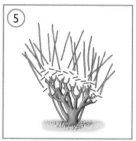

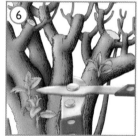

In autumn, after flowering, cut back the faded flower stems to prevent self-seeding and minimise root damage from windrock in winter weather.

THIRD & SUBSEQUENT YEARS
In spring, prune back all the previous year's flowering growth to one or two bud pairs, as in step 3. Repeat this pruning annually.

When the permanent framework becomes overcrowded with branches, remove the oldest ones or misplaced ones with loppers or a saw.

Others, such as late summer- and autumn-flowering ceanothus and Spanish broom (*Spartium*), can be encouraged to produce a very low-lying framework of permanent branches. Shorten their stems to within a few centimetres (inches) of this framework each year.

PRUNING BUDDLEJA DAVIDII

Vigorous summer-flowering shrubs, such as *Buddleja davidii*, blue spiraea (*Caryopteris*) and Russian sage (*Perovskia*), should be encouraged to form a permanent woody framework and the previous year's growth cut back hard to this framework annually.

HARD PRUNING FOR COLOURFUL STEMS

A few deciduous shrubs, such as dogwood (*Cornus*), ornamental brambles (*Rubus*) and willow (*Salix*), are grown for their colourful stems, which are particularly noticeable during the winter months. However, their colour intensity fades as the stems get older, so it is important to hard prune in spring to ensure plenty of fresh, new growth that will colour up well by the following winter.

This is best carried out annually, although it can be reduced to every two or three years if necessary. If height is needed in the garden throughout spring and early summer, prune hard only one third to one half of the stems each year, and carry out the rest of the pruning over a two- to three-year period, removing the oldest stems each year.

Hard pruning may reduce flowering of dogwoods and brambles. Therefore, where flowering is important, carry out pruning over two years, as above.

Using this pruning technique on some dogwoods, such as *Cornus alba* 'Elegantissima', will not only encourage their colourful stems but also enhance the leaf colouring for which they are renowned.

The practice of cutting back hard to ground level is also known as coppicing

PRUNING DOGWOOD

FIRST YEAR
After planting from autumn to spring, prune back hard all stems close to their base.

Vigorous new stems, with the best colouring, form during late spring and summer.

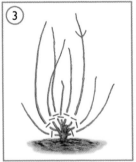

SECOND &
SUBSEQUENT YEARS
Prune back all stems hard, as in step 1. Remove weak and old stumps.

Catalpa bignonioides *'Aurea' produces stronger leaf colour when pruned.*

(see p70). In addition, dogwoods and willows can be pollarded, where the stems are grown on top of a trunk, the height of which can be varied to your own needs (see p71).

HARD PRUNING FOR COLOURFUL FOLIAGE

Several deciduous shrubs and trees are sometimes cultivated mainly for their colourful foliage; good examples include Indian bean tree (*Catalpa bignonioides*), purple-leaved hazel (*Corylus maxima* 'Purpurea'), smoke bush (*Cotinus*), foxglove tree (*Paulownia tomentosa*), sumach (*Rhus typhina*) and various elders (*Sambucus*).

These shrubs will produce larger and more colourful leaves if hard pruned annually in spring. The technique is the same as for pruning for winter stems (see opposite) or hard pruning (see p42), that is cutting back hard the stems produced the previous year.

45

Unfortunately, this hard pruning will more or less prevent the plants flowering, which for most of these shrubs is of no consequence. If you do want the plants to flower (such as with Indian bean tree, purple-leaved hazel, smoke bush, foxglove tree and sumach), you must prune less harshly or, in the case of smoke bush, revert to minimal pruning (see p40). A different, and better, approach is to prune one third or one half of the stems each year. Those that are pruned will produce the better foliage, while those left unpruned will produce flowers.

• PRUNING EVERGREEN SHRUBS •

FORMATIVE PRUNING

Young evergreen shrubs may sometimes need initial training to help them develop a main stem or strong, bushy growth (see p13). In some cases, it may be necessary to prevent competition for the main stem from upper sideshoots. In others, where the main stem is weak or spindly with few branches, pruning will encourage new sideshoots.

RENEWAL PRUNING

Providing evergreen shrubs have been given any necessary formative pruning when young, to create a well-balanced framework of branches (see left), they generally need the minimum of pruning in subsequent years.

Careful deadheading after flowering, to remove the faded flowerheads, will prevent the plant unnecessarily

REMOVING A
DUAL LEADER

STIMULATING
SIDESHOOTS

In spring, prune back sideshoots that compete with the main stem. Double or even triple main stems will spoil the look of the shrub and can be weak points that become damaged in windy conditions.

In spring, cut back the tip of the main stem by up to five leaves or back to strong growth to stimulate the development of sideshoots from growth buds in the leaf axils (see inset).

Throughout summer, new sideshoots will form to produce a much bushier plant. The top sideshoot may need training to take over as the main shoot and continue the upward growth.

Gum (Eucalyptus) *can be hard pruned and grown as a shrub.*

diverting energy into seed production and can help tidy up and improve the look of the plant. However, this may not be possible on large shrubs.

Always remove any wayward or unwanted stems and dying, dead, diseased or damaged growth, especially after a harsh winter. Although it is preferable to do this job as soon as the problem is spotted, the optimum time to do it is in spring, to give the plant plenty of time for wounds to heal and regrowth to ripen before cooler weather in autumn and winter. But bear in mind that spring-flowering shrubs flower on growth produced the previous year, so pruning before flowering will remove the flower buds. Also, pruning too early in the year will produce wounds and young growth that may be susceptible to heavy frost damage. Pruning much later in the year, such as late summer or autumn, produces soft growth that

will not have time to harden before winter and so is also more susceptible to damage from cold weather.

HARD PRUNING

Some evergreens, grown purely for their foliage, can be cut back hard to improve their foliage effect (see p45). This is particularly true of gum (*Eucalyptus*), which produces attractive, rounded juvenile foliage on new growth and less decorative, willow-like growth on old stems. Prune it to ground level annually.

• MINIMAL EVERGREEN PRUNING •

Some evergreen shrubs positively hate being pruned hard once established, as they do not readily reshoot from old wood. These include brooms (*Cytisus* and *Genista*), heathers (*Calluna* and *Erica*), lavender, rosemary and thyme.

Lightly prune or trim these plants annually to keep them strong, bushy and flowering well. If you leave them for several years and then prune into old, hard, brown wood these plants will die or produce very poor, weak, spindly regrowth that never performs well. Old and neglected plants that have grown too tall, look unsightly or are not producing good displays are best replaced, rather than trying to rejuvenate them.

LAVENDERS

These plants often benefit from trimming twice a year to keep them compact, bushy and flowering well. If not pruned regularly in this way, lavender will produce lots of tall, leggy, woody stems, which are difficult to keep looking good. Never cut into the older,

PRUNING LAVENDER

FIRST YEAR
In midspring, cut back young plants quite hard, removing spindly and untidy growth, to encourage new growth and to start creating a bushy shape.

After flowering, remove the faded flowerheads by giving the plant a light trim with shears. Do not prune hard, but you can remove some of the top leaves.

SECOND &
SUBSEQUENT
YEARS
In midspring, trim with shears. If needed, you can cut back quite hard, but do not cut into older, leafless growth as this will not regenerate.

After several years, the plant may become spindly and top heavy, despite annual trimming. Eventually, it will need replacing, as will badly shaped plants.

Annual light pruning will keep lavender plants bushy and flowering well.

leafless stems. Because lavenders, especially French lavender (*L. stoechas* and *L. dentata*), can be damaged by cold and frost, prune only in spring and summer.

HEATHERS

These need only minimal trimming over. This keeps plants bushy, vigorous and flowering well. Trim the winter- and spring-flowering types in spring, once they have finished flowering. Summer- and autumn-flowering varieties can either be trimmed after flowering or in spring if you want to keep the ornamental faded heads over winter.

PRUNING HEATHER

Lightly trim over the plant with shears or even scissors on small plants. Aim to remove the faded flowerheads and up to 3cm (1in) of leafy growth.

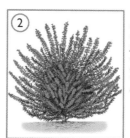

Winter-flowering heathers should be pruned after flowering in spring. Summer- and autumn-flowering varieties can be done at the same time.

• SHRUB RENOVATION •

Shrubs that prefer regular pruning but have been neglected for several years, those that have become too dense in the middle with lots of old branches or shrubs that have grown far too tall for their allotted space can sometimes be rejuvenated. This may be viewed as a better alternative to removing the plant and disposing of it.

This renovation involves very hard and drastic pruning – usually cutting plants down to or just above ground level. Not all plants respond well to this treatment, but most have remarkable recovery powers and can be brought back to productive life again.

Most deciduous shrubs will come back to productivity really well. Evergreens are far more variable. Those evergreen shrubs that do not respond well to hard pruning, and the vast majority of conifers cannot be renovated. On the other hand, camellia, cherry laurel (*Prunus laurocerasus*), holly (*Ilex*), firethorn (*Pyracantha*), rhododendron and yew (*Taxus baccata*) all recover remarkably rapidly from renovation and soon settle back into normal growth.

Deciduous shrubs that do not respond well to such drastic treatment when done all at once often do better if the treatment is carried out over two or

REJUVENATING A DECIDUOUS SHRUB OVER ONE YEAR

In winter, cut back all stems to within 15–30cm (6–12in) of ground level. Feed and mulch.

Remove excessive regrowth by cutting out the thinnest, new shoots to leave the strongest ones.

REJUVENATING A DECIDUOUS SHRUB OVER TWO YEARS

FIRST YEAR
In winter, cut back half of the stems to ground level, starting with the oldest.

By summer, new stems will have grown from the pruned stems, and the old stems will have flowered normally.

SECOND YEAR
In winter, remove the other half of old stems not pruned in the first year.

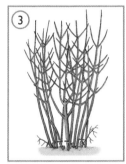

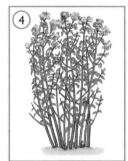

By summer, new stems will have grown from the cut base, and the stems pruned in the first year will have flowered.

three years – by cutting back either one half or one third of the stems each year. Evergreens, however, should be renovated in one go as long-term pruning over a few years produces an uneven, untidy and unsightly plant.

Rejuvenate deciduous shrubs when dormant in winter, while evergreens are best left until late spring when they are just breaking into growth.

If drastic renovation does not work, then the plant should be replaced.

AFTERCARE

As renovation is a shock for a plant and a lot of woody material is removed, shrubs treated in this way must be given a generous feed of a balanced, granular fertiliser. Water this in well, and mulch the soil to maintain soil moisture and keep weeds at bay.

Repeat such feeding and mulching every spring, until the shrub is back to its former glory, which normally takes three or four years.

• TOPIARY MASTERCLASS •

The fine branch structure of box (*Buxus sempervirens*) and its small leaves make it an ideal shrub for topiary and mean that it can be trained into a wide range of shapes and forms – from simple balls and pyramids to more intricate shapes.

Other evergreen shrubs, such as yew (*Taxus baccata*), holly (*Ilex*), myrtle (*Myrtus*) and privet (*Ligustrum*), that have similar form and small leaves are also suitable.

TOPIARY

Decide on the shape you want to create – balls, pyramids and cones are the easiest shapes to start with.

Allow the plant to grow to the required height before removing the main leading shoot. Then begin clipping the plant into shape. You can do this by eye or else make a template or a wooden frame to ensure the shape is clipped uniformly over the plant.

As the plant matures it will bush out and the branches and leaves will knit together to give a solid appearance. This process can take many years, depending on the plant selected and the ultimate size required.

To maintain your topiary shape, trim it once or twice a year.

TOPIARY FRAMES

For more intricate topiary shapes, frames are available. These are placed over the plant in the early stages of growth, allowing the plant to fill the frame to create the desired shape. Once the plant starts to protrude through the frame, prune to maintain the shape of the frame.

CLOUD PRUNING

This Oriental method of pruning trees and shrubs emphasises the plant's form and branch structure. The plants are pruned to reveal the stems with the remaining foliage sculpted into rounded shapes or 'clouds'. As well as box, small-leaved Japanese privet (*Ligustrum japonicum*), pine (*Pinus*) and yew make good choices for cloud pruning.

Select a suitable plant that has an interesting formation of branches, because these will form the basis of the design. The branches do not have to be symmetrical and equal in size, but you do need to plan ahead, and work out which branches you want to keep and how you want the plant to look when it has been 'finished'.

Ideally, make the cuts when the plant is young, because the pruning cuts will

disappear as the plant matures. Remove unwanted branches and twigs from the centre of the plant, so that the main branches are bare, and manipulate the branches by using stakes or weights to get the shapes you want. If you wish

Topiary shapes provide lots of garden interest and structure.

your plant to continue to grow taller and wider, do not prune the growing tips on the ends of the branches.

Topiary pyramid

Topiary ball

Cloud-pruned shrub

Parterre

Standard shrub

54

Once you have the desired length and height, trim the tips and this will encourage branching and the cloud shape will begin to fill out.

In summer, trim the clouds with secateurs or shears to keep the plant in shape and ensure the branches remain clear of growth. Remove suckers (see p69) and unwanted branches at the same time. Fast-growing species, such as Japanese privet, may need to be trimmed several times a year.

PARTERRES

Parterres are a style of beautifully ornate clipped box hedges created in mirrored patterns or geometric designs. In traditional parterre gardens, the gaps in the patterns are left open and the ground covered with ornamental gravel, to produce a crisp, clean effect. Styles are now more elaborate, and low-growing and dwarf plants are added to the ground between the parterres to give extra colour and interest.

TRAINING STANDARDS

A wide range of shrubs can be trained as standards, which are plants with a clear, single stem and a bushy head. Such plants give height to a border and raise the plant's decorative features to eye level, where they are more likely to be better enjoyed.

Standards need staking in their formative years. A bamboo cane is usually sufficient initially, but a wooden stake may be required as the plant gets older, depending on the size and weight of the head. Some standards need permanent staking.

Select a plant with a single, strong shoot or leader, or prune away any other shoots to provide a single leader. Keep the leader growing well, removing sideshoots as they form but keeping all leaves that grow on the leader, until it is slightly taller than the desired height. Then pinch out the growing point; this will induce the buds below to break and start forming the branches of the head.

Allow the sideshoots in the head to grow for one year, and then reduce them by half. Once sideshoots start to form on these shoots they too can be cut back to start developing a bushy head.

When the head has formed, carry out further pruning as normal for that plant, following the information in the pruning directory (see p162), to keep the head bushy and the plant flowering or fruiting as expected. Remove sideshoots on the main stem or, better still, rub them out as buds, as soon as possible.

ORNAMENTAL TREES

• INTRODUCTION •

A well-grown tree makes a superb focal point in any garden. It provides structure and leaf canopy, but may also boast unusually coloured foliage, or foliage that turns beautiful colours in autumn. Other trees produce fruit in autumn and winter and yet others have coloured and ornamental bark.

When choosing a tree, take into account its final height. Many trees are suitable for even the smallest garden. But where a large tree has been chosen (or inherited when moving into a house with an established garden) and has outgrown its position, you will spoil its shape and form by constantly 'butchering' it to keep it within bounds. Such pruning might even be illegal if the tree is protected by a tree preservation order (see p81).

Most young trees supplied by nurseries and garden centres have already had their initial training, but whips (see p27) and other very young trees usually need formative training if they are to achieve the desired shape and overall effect.

Once established, many trees require little or no further pruning, apart from removing dead, dying, damaged, diseased or unwanted growth that spoils the tree's overall shape and appearance.

FORMATIVE PRUNING

Some trees naturally develop a well-shaped branch structure. Others will benefit from some initial pruning, especially if they need only minimal pruning when mature.

Untrained whips and feathered whips will definitely require formative pruning to build up a good branch structure.

First year

During its first year a whip produces leaves and often small shoots along the main stem. Do not remove these because the tree needs them to grow as much as possible.

In winter, cut off very weak or wayward growth. If the leading shoot is growing poorly, replace it by cutting it back to the next young shoot or a strong bud. Train the replacement shoot upwards to take over as the new leader. Remove laterals that compete with the leader. Other than that, the whip will not need any other formative pruning.

Second year

As the young tree develops strong laterals along its main stem, continue to remove any competing laterals and growth that is dead or damaged.

It is important to maintain strong main or leading shoots that will eventually form the main trunk for your tree. If competing leaders are not dealt with early, they are likely to cause problems from crossing branches and an unsound main branch framework later on.

Formative pruning of young trees will produce better structure when mature.

Subsequent years

Most trees are grown as feathered trees (see p62) or branch-headed trees (see p64) and their further formative pruning is dealt with on these pages.

Different tree species naturally grow to a certain, predetermined shape. This not only affects how it looks ornamentally in the garden but also, in many cases, how it should be trained and pruned. It is, therefore, important to recognise its overall shape and growth pattern.

FEATHERED TREE

Some tree species naturally retain their lower branches, rather than losing them and developing into standards: for example, silver birch (*Betula pendula*) and most conifers. The main trunk may be clothed in branches right down to ground level (see p62).

BRANCH-HEADED STANDARD

These trees have a single, clear trunk, which then branches to form a head or crown. It happens naturally in many trees, and can also be produced by cutting back a young tree's main stem (see p64) to stimulate branching, or by grafting the species or variety onto a rootstock, such as in some cherries (*Prunus*). Any lower branches on the main stem should then be removed.

Half-standards, with 1–1.2m (3–4ft) of clear stem, are often more suitable for less vigorous, lower-growing species.

CENTRAL-LEADER STANDARD

The main trunk of these trees persists throughout their length, terminating in a distinct leading shoot. Some trees grow naturally like this, whereas others can be produced by gradually removing lower branches over a number of years to leave a clear trunk.

As with branch-headed standards (see left), the clear trunk can be anything from 1m (3ft) for small trees to 3m (10ft) for very vigorous, tall tree species; in most cases you can decide exactly how clear you want the trunk to be.

WEEPING TREE

Weeping standards either form naturally, such as weeping willow (*Salix babylonica*), or are produced by grafting a weeping or prostrate variety onto a suitable stem. Others, such as weeping birch (*Betula pendula* 'Youngii'), naturally form weeping, feathered trees, although the lower branches on the main stem are usually removed to show off the trunk to its best advantage.

FASTIGIATE TREE

These are narrow, columnar trees with short or even upward-growing branches that often completely clothe the main

60

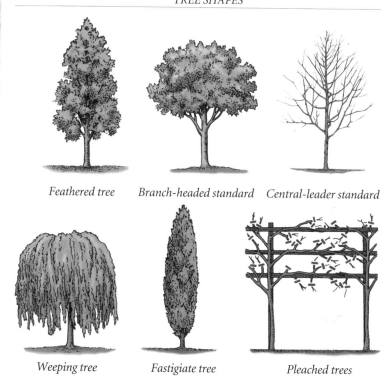

TREE SHAPES

Feathered tree Branch-headed standard Central-leader standard

Weeping tree Fastigiate tree Pleached trees

trunk. It is a natural habit and cannot be produced by training and pruning.

MULTISTEMMED TREE

Trees or large shrubs can be pruned and trained to produce several main stems coming from ground level or above a very short stem, or leg, just above ground level. Some multistemmed trees arise from suckers (see p69).

PLEACHING

Pleaching is a specialised ornamental growing method that involves weaving together the branches of a row of trees, then regular, formal pruning to produce a hedge or barrier 'on stilts'. It is suitable for hornbeam (*Carpinus*), hawthorn (*Crataegus*), holly (*Ilex*), willow (*Salix*) and lime (*Tilia*). Such a feature takes several years to produce (see p72).

• FEATHERED TREES •

Although the natural form of most young trees is to have their main stem clothed in evenly spaced branches almost down to ground level, only some trees retain their lower branches when they mature: for example, alder (*Alnus*), birch (*Betula*), hornbeam (*Carpinus*), holm oak (*Quercus ilex*), mountain ash or rowan (*Sorbus aucuparia*), most conifers and many evergreen trees.

Such feathered trees are the easiest to train into attractive mature specimens. Simply remove any sideshoots that are not well spaced to produce a balanced tree and cut out any branches that have a narrow angle of attachment to the main stem; these may be damaged in strong winds when older and heavier (see p67).

You may need to prune a young or untrained tree early on so it develops a single, dominant main stem, or leader. At all costs, you must prevent the tree forming a forked or double leader, by removing any competing stems that may form near the top of the tree (see step 3 below). A forked leader will not

PRUNING A FEATHERED TREE

FIRST YEAR
At planting time, stake and tie the tree and allow it to grow without pruning during its first spring and summer.

In mid- to late autumn, remove any shoots that have developed close to the base, otherwise they may rival the main stem.

SECOND YEAR
In spring or summer, remove any sideshoots that grow upwards and compete with the leading stem. Remove the stake after 18 months.

only spoil the shape but it will also be weak and easily damaged by strong winds. Strong stems that grow at the base of the tree should similarly be removed, otherwise there is a chance of producing a multistemmed tree.

As the tree matures over the following years, it should naturally form a symmetrical, almost pyramidal shape, on its own. However, you can help encourage this by removing any branches that ruin the symmetry or that cross from one side of the tree to the other. On deciduous trees, this can be done from late autumn to winter, once the tree has dropped its leaves. Conifers are best treated in spring or summer.

Lower branches that may get in the way, for example preventing mowing if the tree is planted in the lawn, or that are growing too thickly or are overcrowded can be removed at the same time.

Feathered trees of some species, such as rowans, can be converted into central-leader standard trees (see p65), by cutting back the lower branches over several years until the required height of bare main trunk has been reached.

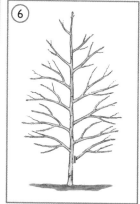

In spring or summer, remove any very low branches because these may get in the way later on and spoil the shape of the tree.

THIRD YEAR
In winter, remove any upper shoots that may get in the way and interfere with the leading stem.

FOURTH &
SUBSEQUENT YEARS
Allow the tree to develop naturally, but remove badly placed branches in autumn or winter.

• BRANCH-HEADED STANDARDS •

This shape is one of the commonest ones for a wide range of ornamental garden trees, especially cherry (*Prunus*), crab apple (*Malus*), poplar (*Populus*) and hawthorn (*Crataegus*).

The head or crown is made up of lots of preferably equally spaced, main branches. These can start naturally at any height from ground level, and mainly depend on the vigour of the species involved; alternatively, lower branches can be removed early in the tree's life if a higher crown is required. Branch-headed standards, therefore, do not have a dominant central leading trunk (see box right).

Early training of a branch-headed standard may be needed, depending on the age, size and amount of training the tree has already received when purchased. Such formative pruning involves removing the lowest side

PRUNING A BRANCH-HEADED STANDARD

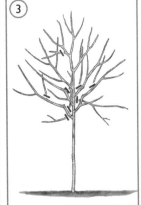

FIRST YEAR
At the time of planting, stake and tie the tree and allow it to grow without pruning in its first spring and summer. Remove any shoots that appear on the main stem while young, before they can develop further.

SECOND & SUBSEQUENT YEARS
Allow branches to grow at the head of the tree to develop the crown. In spring or summer, if a leading shoot develops, cut it back to a strong bud to encourage further branching in the crown.

In autumn, cut out crossing, overcrowded or low branches to form an open, evenly spaced framework in the crown. Remove any shoots that appear on the main stem below the crown.

Crab apples (Malus) *look great when grown as branch-headed trees.*

branches until the required length of clear trunk has been reached.

Once the required length of clear trunk has been achieved, minimal further pruning is needed other than to improve the shape and symmetry of the tree by removing badly placed or crossing branches in the crown. And, of course, dead, diseased or damaged branches should be removed as soon as they appear. You should aim to create an open crown framework of healthy, well-spaced branches, so cut out any that cause overcrowding.

Also, in the early years, look out for vigorous upright shoots that form within the crown as these may develop into dominant leaders, which will take over and spoil the shape of the tree. Similarly, weak V-shaped branch junctions and steep branches may need removing (see p67).

Shorter half-standards are often a more suitable choice for less vigorous, lower-growing species.

PRUNING A CENTRAL-LEADER STANDARD

This form of branch structure and shape is best suited to large trees. You should formative prune as for feathered trees (see p62) and then gradually remove lower branches each year as required until the desired clear trunk is achieved.

• REMOVING LARGE & DIFFERENT BRANCH TYPES •

Sometimes it may be necessary to remove very large branches from established trees. This has to be done carefully to ensure the weight of the branch does not cause major bark ripping and extensive damage to the main trunk or other large branches as the branch comes away from the tree.

If you are in any doubt as to whether such pruning is beyond your capabilities, you should always seek the advice of a fully qualified and insured tree surgeon.

SAFETY

If you do decide to tackle the job yourself, you must remember that pruning large branches can also be potentially dangerous both to you and surrounding property.

When using a ladder to prune a tall tree, ensure it is stable and firmly attached to the tree and preferably have someone hold the bottom of the ladder. If you are doing a lot of pruning, it may be worth using scaffolding or a scaffold platform, which is safer than a ladder.

REMOVING A LARGE BRANCH

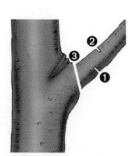

Start by sawing through the underside of the branch, or final section of a very large branch, up to about 30cm (12in) away from the main stem or trunk, cutting to about one quarter of its depth ❶; *this will prevent any bark tearing should the branch break. Then cut right through the branch from the top* ❷, *a few centimetres beyond the first undercut. The remaining stub will now be more manageable and allow you to make a careful, clean cut following the line of the branch collar* ❸. *Then smooth away any rough edges that remain.*

WHERE TO CUT ON DIFFERENT TYPES OF BRANCHES

Some types of branches need to be removed to maintain a tree's shape and its health. Steep and V-shaped branches, for example, can be very weak and can snap under their weight or in windy conditions.

Where there is a swollen branch collar and raised bark ridge, above the branch, prune outside the collar and ridge.

If there is no obvious branch collar, cut along an angled line starting from the outer edge of the bark ridge, running away from the trunk.

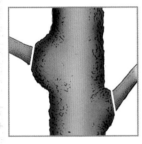

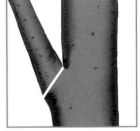

Obvious ridges and collars make branch removal straightforward. Cut just beyond the bark ridge and the swollen branch collar.

Remove V-shaped branch junctions because they are very weak. Cut from below the branch to avoid damaging the trunk.

Steep branches may need removing and should be cut from below. Prune carefully without cutting anything from the trunk.

LARGE BRANCHES

Large pruning cuts can take several years to heal and are potential entry points for disease, which can lead to severe rotting. So, it is important to make clean cuts with sharp tools because these heal the quickest. Also, after pruning, make sure you smooth any residual rough surfaces with a pruning knife or, in some cases, using a chisel or fine saw.

In addition, it is important to make the pruning cut in the right place. Always cut so that the branch collar (the ring of swelling at its base) – if it exists – and the bark ridge are left intact. Wounds heal much quicker if large branches are removed in this way. Never cut a branch flush to the main stem or trunk.

It may be easier to remove a large branch in small, manageable sections.

• REMOVING UNWANTED GROWTH •

There are several types of unwanted growth on trees and shrubs: for example, water shoots, suckers and reverted growth. These should be removed as soon as they are seen. If left too long, they can become difficult to remove properly and cleanly.

WATER SHOOTS

In some trees, several buds break at the same point and time, usually after severe pruning or around old wounds, producing a thicket of thin stems called water shoots. In time, these may produce useful stem regrowth and go on to flower and fruit normally, but they are usually so numerous that they crowd one another and may ruin the shape of the plant. In such cases they should either be thinned out or be removed completely if not needed to produce replacement growth.

DEALING WITH WATER SHOOTS

Clusters of thin shoots appear on trunks and main branches, often around old pruning wounds. Cut them out completely, back to their base, as they may also weaken other growth. With a thumb, 'rub out' any unwanted buds at the same time.

PULLING AWAY SUCKERS

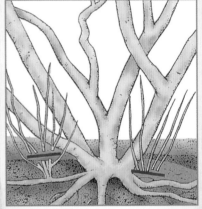

The best way to remove suckers is to trace them back to where they join the main root and then carefully tear them off (right) – usually with a sharp jerking motion to prevent tearing the root's bark. Cutting them off (left) leaves behind dormant buds that will reshoot to produce further suckers; pulling away the suckers removes these buds.

Variegated elaeagnus often produce shoots with all-green, reverted growth.

SUCKERS

A sucker is a shoot that arises at or below ground level from the roots or underground stems.

Some plants are grafted onto rootstocks to control their growth, in which case suckers are shoots that arise from below the graft union, that is, where the cultivated plant was grafted onto the rootstock. On standard trees and roses this may even be on the main stem. On all grafted plants, remove any suckers that arise from the rootstock, as they are usually very vigorous and may take over and eventually dominate the top growth.

Some shrubs are grown as multistemmed thickets, where each stem arises from suckers. In these cases, the suckers are useful, but stems may need thinning out to prevent thick growth. Trees such as sumachs (*Rhus*) and cherries have roots from which new shoots appear a long way from the main plant and these will need to be removed.

69

REVERTED GROWTH

Plants that are grown for their variegated or otherwise coloured leaves often produce stems whose foliage is all green; this is called reversion. Others that are grown for their curly or twisted stems may produce straight stems. In both cases, prune out the aberrant stem as soon as it is spotted, cutting the stem right back to where it originated.

Reverted stems are generally more vigorous and, if left, will soon take over the rest of the plant, thereby spoiling its overall appearance.

• OTHER TREE-PRUNING TECHNIQUES •

In addition to general pruning, there are a few more specialised pruning techniques that may prove useful: coppicing, pollarding, pleaching (see p72), crown pruning (see p73), root pruning (see p74) and bark ringing (see p76).

COPPICING

Coppicing, also known as stooling, is the technique of cutting back the stems of shrubs and trees to just above ground level to encourage new, stronger shoots to form. It is particularly useful to promote colourful juvenile stems and ornamental foliage (see p44) and to rejuvenate plants that tolerate hard pruning (see p50).

Overgrown hazel (*Corylus*), hornbeam (*Carpinus*) and yew (*Taxus baccata*) – one of the few conifer species that will tolerate hard pruning – can be cut close to the ground in late winter. This results in the production of lots of new stems that can be thinned out to make an open, more airy bush. Hazels, in particular, are coppiced every few years to produce long, straight stems, and these can be used as plant supports in the garden.

If necessary, after coppicing, it is sometimes possible to select a

COPPICING A TREE

Select a suitable large or overgrown tree that is suitable for coppicing.

In winter or early spring, cut down all stems close to their base. Feed the plant generously.

During spring and summer, new shoots will rapidly grow from the resulting stool.

single stem and grow it on to form a replacement leader from which to retrain and develop a new crown.

Coppicing is a very severe, but useful, way of keeping some trees that naturally grow tall within bounds. Foxglove tree (*Paulownia tomentosa*), for example, can reach 25m (80ft) high but coppicing will keep it to a large shrub, which can easily grow 3m (10ft) in a single year. Gum (*Eucalyptus*) trees can be treated similarly, especially as tall trees are very susceptible to windrock and being blown down in strong winds.

Because coppicing helps produce better foliage colour, it is useful when growing trees with colourful foliage, such as *Acer negundo* 'Flamingo', *A. negundo* 'Kelly's Gold and *Populus* × *canadensis* 'Aurea'.

Slightly tender evergreens, such as bay (*Laurus nobilis*) and gum, may be damaged in severe winters and are easier to protect with fleece or similar covers when coppiced, and so kept smaller than they would naturally grow.

Another reason for coppicing is to produce a bushy, multistemmed effect for tree species used for hedging, such as beech (*Fagus*), box elder (*Acer negundo*), field maple (*Acer campestre*), hawthorn (*Crataegus*), hazel, hornbeam and yew.

POLLARDING A TREE

In late winter or early spring, cut the stems back hard to near their base, so a framework of stems can develop from the trunk.

POLLARDING

Pollarding is similar to coppicing (see left), except that the framework of stems is produced on the top of a single trunk. This allows you to have the effect of coppicing but at a greater height above ground level. As a result, pollarded trees and shrubs can be used as taller structural features in a garden.

This technique is also useful for restricting the height of certain trees that will tolerate the hard pruning necessary to create the pollard effect.

Trees that respond well to pollarding include some species of maple (*Acer*), alder (*Alnus*), ash (*Fraxinus*), oak (*Quercus*), tulip tree (*Liriodendron*), walnut (*Morus*), plane (*Platanus*), lime (*Tilia*) and elm (*Ulmus*).

Hard pruning is essential for successful pollarding.

Pollarding is best started on young trees as young wood heals rapidly, reducing the risk of decay. Initially, allow the tree to grow to the desired height, after which the branch framework is produced in the same way as coppicing.

The best time for pollarding is in late winter or early spring. Cut stems above the previous pollarding cuts, in order to avoid exposing older wood, which may be at an increased risk of decay.

Once pollarded, it is important to continue the cycle of cutting as the weight and angle of the new branches can lead to weakness, particularly where many stems are crowded together,

PLEACHING

Plant young, whippy trees, 1.2m (4ft) apart, in winter. In summer, train and tie in new shoots to a support framework of stakes and horizontal wires. Plait the sideshoots with neighbouring ones.

In autumn or winter, cut unwanted, outward-growing shoots back to one or two buds from the base. Pinch out the leading stems when they have reached the required height.

When the main branch system has been formed, shorten all shoot growth annually in summer, to retain the shape and encourage bushy growth.

In this garden, Acer platanoides *'Drummondii' has been pleached to form an attractive, eye-catching feature.*

CROWN
THINNING
*This allows more
light through the
canopy, reducing
shading below and
wind resistance.*

CROWN LIFTING
*Removing lower
branches will lift
the crown of the
tree to provide more
ground clearance.*

CROWN PRUNING

Trees with a dense canopy or whose lower branches are too low may need major surgery. This may simply be to reduce the amount of shade the tree casts or to improve air flow and so minimise disease. On large trees such major operations are best tackled by a qualified tree surgeon.

Crown thinning

Thinning increases light penetration and reduces wind resistance by the selective removal of branches throughout the canopy. This improves the tree's strength against adverse weather conditions as the wind can more readily pass through.

Crown reduction

This reduces the overall size of the crown, while maintaining its natural shape. Crown reduction is often used where part of a tree touches, or is very close to, a building, in which case only part of the crown or specific branches are shortened.

It may be better to carry out crown thinning and reduction over two years.

Crown lifting

The selective removal of the lower branches by crown lifting will increase the distance between the base of the canopy and ground level. This type of pruning should, if possible, be carried out before the tree reaches maturity in order to avoid large wounds. Crown lifting allows more light through the canopy and can help prevent low-lying obstructions. For best results, you should not lift lower branches to more than one third of the tree's total height.

73

ROOT PRUNING

Pruning plant roots may sound an unusual suggestion and even a drastic one, but in some circumstances it is useful. Root pruning works because it reduces a plant's vigour by slowing down and restraining excessive top growth and so promotes the formation of flowering growth instead of leafy growth. Thus it can bring trees and shrubs into flower and fruit when less severe pruning measures have been ineffective. It is an invaluable technique for unproductive fruit trees.

Root pruning is best carried out from autumn to late winter, when the tree is fully dormant. Dig up very young trees – up to five years old – and replant in the same position or a more suitable one. The tree will probably need to be restaked for the first couple of years while it re-establishes. Water it well in summer.

For slightly older trees, dig a trench around the tree, 30–45cm (12–18in) deep and wide, and 1.2–1.5m (4–5ft) from the trunk. Then saw through the major roots. Refill the trench as soon as possible to prevent the roots drying out excessively, stake the tree, if appropriate, and water it well in the following two or three summers.

PRUNING A TREE'S ROOTS

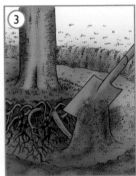

When the tree is dormant, mark out and then dig out a trench around the tree, 1.2–1.5m (4–5ft) from its trunk.

Carefully fold or tuck away the fibrous roots to expose thicker, woodier ones. Cut these woody roots back with a pruning saw.

Retain the thinner, fibrous roots and spread them back into the trench. Refill the trench and firm down the soil.

Root pruning is a drastic method of reducing growth and promoting flowering.

Root slicing

A milder pruning effect, and one that is more suitable for small trees, shrubs and even climbers, can be achieved by inserting a spade's blade to its full depth around the plant to cut the surface roots. Make the cut in a circle at the spread of the plant's branches. If this does not reduce the plant's vigour and encourage flowering and fruiting, repeat the root slicing the following year, but work more closely to the plant.

Root pruning of well-established trees and old, large shrubs is probably best carried out over two years, removing half the roots at a time.

Very old and mature plants should not be root pruned, except as a very last resort, as they have less resilience than younger ones.

Pot-grown plants

Plants growing in containers are easily root pruned. Shorten up to 20 percent of the roots by about one quarter, and trim the other roots to ensure the plant will fit back into the same pot. Then replant with fresh potting compost to which controlled-release fertiliser has been added. Water well.

BARK RINGING

Sometimes called girdling, bark ringing has a similar effect to root pruning (see p74), in that it can curb excessive leafy growth and help promote flowering and fruiting. It is a very good technique for unproductive fruit trees, although it is not suitable for stone fruit trees, such as plums and cherries, as it can lead to disease problems. It should be used only on very vigorous trees.

Bark ringing works by disrupting the flow of sugars and other nutrients to the roots, and thereby checking the growth of the roots and hence the whole tree.

However, this technique should really be used only as a last resort and must be carried out correctly or the tree can be damaged or even killed.

Bark ringing can reduce excessive leafy growth and help promote flowering.

(1)	(2)	(3)

In spring, mark out a ring, 6–13mm (¼–½in) wide, on the main trunk using string or tape as a guide. Make deep, parallel cuts at both edges for most of the ring.

Carefully and cleanly remove the resulting circle of bark, levering it up and out. Either complete the circle or leave 3cm (1in) of the ring untouched.

Cover the wound with overlapping bindings of insulating tape or adhesive tape. Smear the edge of the tape with petroleum jelly to exclude air.

Carry out bark ringing in mid- to late spring. If the process needs to be repeated, wait a couple of years before doing it again.

You will need a very sharp knife, although a chisel can be used with care on trees with tough bark.

Cut the ring at a suitable height above ground level, but well below the lowest branches. A ring 6mm (¼in) wide is suitable for most trees, increasing this to 13mm (½in) for large trees. Ensure the cut penetrates right through the bark and cambium layer, into the woody interior of the branch.

Although it is usually recommended that the whole ring is removed entirely, a section 3cm (1in) long can be left if you are at all worried that a complete ring may damage/kill the tree and it will help give you some peace of mind. Leaving a section of the bark ring in place will, however, reduce the overall effect of this pruning method and will not slow down growth as successfully.

Cover the resulting wound with insulating tape, adhesive tape or similar, but do not poke the tape into the cut surface. Finally, seal the tape edges with petroleum jelly or grafting wax to exclude air, pests, diseases and to aid rapid healing by preventing the wound drying out. Remove the tape once scar tissue has begun to form on the wound.

• TREE RENOVATION •

Trees that have been left to grow for many years without any pruning may need major renovation to bring them back to their former glory.

Very large trees are best left to a qualified tree surgeon, who will have a better idea of how to tackle what is a major pruning project. Such a professional will also have the correct tools – including safety equipment – to carry out the work high in the crown.

Smaller trees can usually be tackled by home gardeners. For best results, carry out such tree renovations over two or, better still, three years.

Most tree species are best rejuvenated in late autumn and winter. However, for trees that do not like to be pruned when dormant, such as cherry – both ornamental and edible varieties – work

should be carried out in summer. After such severe pruning, it is essential to feed and mulch the tree to help it recover.

CORRECTIVE PRUNING

When carrying out tree renovation, you are more likely to make fewer, larger cuts, removing larger branches (see p66), rather than lots of smaller cuts, so your main tools will be saws and loppers rather than a pair of secateurs.

Start by cutting out all dead, diseased and damaged branches, including those rubbing together. Then prune out branches that are crossing across the centre of the tree, and thin out tangled masses of upright branches to open up the centre of the tree. Also remove any branches that grow out too widely and those that are too high or too low.

PRUNING CONGESTED SHOOTS

Major pruning cuts on large branches can cause vigorous shoots to form around the wound for several years after the cut was made. They should be removed as soon as they appear.

Incorrect, or 'haircut', pruning produces congested clusters of small shoots or knobbly spurs. These need to be heavily, but carefully, thinned out over two or more years to reduce their number.

REJUVENATING A TREE

1

2

3

FIRST YEAR
Remove all dead and diseased branches as well as large branches that spoil the symmetry. Cut away growth from the main trunk.

Thin out the crown to remove some overcrowded branches and those crossing the tree, in order to create an open-headed framework.

SECOND & THIRD YEARS
Remove other branches that spoil the symmetry of the tree and continue to thin out overcrowded branches and smaller shoots.

Such hard pruning is likely to result in water shoots (see p68), which should be thinned out regularly.

Trees that have been badly pruned in the past are likely to produce congested clusters of shoots or knobbly spurs (see box left), which also need thinning out after major renovation has been completed.

NEGLECTED FRUIT TREES

Old fruit trees in a poor state of care are often inherited when moving house. They may have a mass of twiggy branches with lots of unhealthy, leafy

growth and poor yields. Their growth may be stunted or they may be overlarge for the garden. See p148 for details on how to rejuvenate such fruit trees.

When renovating an overgrown tree, use a pruning saw to make large cuts.

• TREE PROBLEMS •

There are a number of problems specific to trees that can be resolved by the use of correct pruning.

DAMAGED BRANCHES & BARK

Branches that are partially broken rarely mend if tied back into position – although this depends on how far through the branch the tear has occurred. It is usually better to remove the branch completely, cutting back to a suitable replacement shoot or bud below the damage.

Bark that has been knocked or torn off is likewise unlikely to reunite with the surrounding bark. Therefore, carefully remove the loose bark, clean the edges with a sharp pruning knife and allow the wound to heal naturally.

DEAD & ROTTEN GROWTH

Although it is important to remove dead, diseased, damaged or dying growth from all plants (see p16), this is particularly true of trees – especially large ones. Large branches are very heavy, and if a rotten one falls from a tree it will cause serious damage to other branches – and anything else or any person – below it.

CAVITIES & HOLLOW TRUNKS

Cavities, usually in the trunk, are caused by old or damaged growth rotting away. They rarely cause problems on otherwise healthy trees and should be left alone. Do not clean out, enlarge, drain or plug such holes with materials such as concrete or wound sealants.

BROKEN OR COMPETING LEADERS

When the main leader on a tree dies back or is damaged, cut it back to the nearest strong lateral and train this vertically to take its place.

If no suitable lateral is available, prune to a healthy growth bud and then train the resulting shoot as a leader. If two shoots result, cut out the weakest one.

Where a vigorous upper lateral has grown strongly and starts competing with the main central leader, shorten or completely remove the twin or competing leader.

TREATING PRUNING CUTS

Providing large pruning cuts have been made cleanly and correctly, the wound should heal by itself and there is no need to use a wound sealant.

Large hollows and severe rotting of tree trunks may make a tree unstable.

Such compounds do not assist the plant's healing process and can, in some cases, actually hinder it. Smooth any large cuts with rough, jagged edges, using a pruning knife, at the same time ensuring that you do not enlarge the wound.

For more information on removing very large branches see p66.

TREE PRESERVATION ORDERS (TPOS)

Some trees, especially those in areas of outstanding natural beauty, may be protected by a Tree Preservation Order (TPO). Such an Order makes it illegal to carry out any work on a tree, including pruning it, without first consulting the issuing body.

To find out if a tree is protected, contact your local planning authority, which is usually the local borough or district council.

Tree Preservation Orders: A Guide to the Law and Good Practice, which is the full guide to TPO law and practice, is available from: Communities and Local Government Publications, Cambertown House, Goldthorpe Industrial Estate, Rotherham S63 9BL; tel: 0300 123 1124; www.communities.gov.uk/publications/planningandbuilding/tposguide.

CLIMBERS

• INTRODUCTION •

Climbers and wall shrubs are extremely versatile plants, and so are especially useful in a small garden, where space is at a premium. Making the most of its vertical space allows you to grow a wider range of plants.

Most gardens have walls or fences that look bare without something to cover them, and pergolas, gazebos, rose arches, pillars and wigwams add extra height and interest to every garden. Large trees and shrubs can also benefit from having something that will climb up them, to extend their seasons of interest.

WALLS

Brick walls retain heat, so provide extra warmth and protection for slightly tender climbers and wall shrubs, especially if the wall faces south, west or southwest.

The soil at the base of walls is usually very dry, so make sure to plant well away from the base, and especially any footings or foundations. Such dry

Wisteria needs regular pruning to promote such a magnificent floral display as this.

UNDERSTANDING INDIVIDUAL GROWTH HABITS

Plants that naturally cling do so by holding onto surfaces using their aerial roots or sucker pads. This means no support system is needed. Examples include ivy (Hedera) and Virginia creeper (Parthenocissus).

Twiners climb by means of curling or twining leaf tendrils, leaf stalks or stems. A support system is needed for the plants to climb up. Examples include clematis, honeysuckle (Lonicera) and wisteria.

Scramblers clamber up supports by using hooked thorns or by rapid elongation of their shoots. A strong support system is needed to which the growth can be tied. Examples include roses and potato vine (Solanum).

Some shrubs can be trained against a wall when attached to wires or trellis. Wall training is especially useful for slightly tender plants, such as bottlebrushes (Callistemon).

conditions can also make some plants more prone to diseases such as mildew on roses and clematis. Therefore, always keep the soil and plants well watered.

SUPPORTS

Nearly all climbing plants and wall shrubs, except those that cling naturally, will need some form of support on which to grow.

Climbers that produce substantial stems can be trained on taut, horizontal support wires. Use vine eyes to hold the wires 5cm (2in) away from the vertical surface, to provide room for the stems to grow and allow air to circulate behind the plant, to minimise diseases. Space the wires 25–45cm (10–18in) apart, depending on the climber, how strong its stems are and how vigorous it is.

Twiners and even scramblers and those plants with thinner or weaker stems, such as clematis and honeysuckle (Lonicera), will do far better if trained up wooden trellis or plastic mesh or netting, as this gives them more places to attach and hang on to. Fix the trellis or netting to wooden battens so there is a gap of 5cm (2in) between the wall surface and the support.

• PRUNING CLIMBERS
& WALL PLANTS •

To ensure climbers and wall shrubs cover their support evenly and perform well, some initial training is usually needed, followed by annual pruning once the plant has a well-balanced framework, if appropriate.

Clematis looks fantastic when trained through other plants or a support.

FORMATIVE TRAINING

Initial training is especially important for those plants that produce a woody framework, such as trumpet vine (*Campsis*) and wisteria, whose sideshoots are thereafter pruned annually to encourage flowering.

Rampant climbers benefit from initial training and regular pruning to ensure they do not just become an unattractive mass of tangled stems that flower poorly.

Start by tying in growth to cover the support evenly and prune back strong growth to keep it within bounds and to encourage sideshoots that will fill in any gaps in the coverage.

Training branches horizontally or in a fan shape, rather than allowing them to grow straight up, encourages better flower displays. This training restricts the flow of sap in the plant and consequently helps initiate flower buds. On walls, fences and trellis this is easy to achieve, while on narrow supports, such as posts, pillars or wigwams, you should twine climbers around the support in a spiral shape.

PRUNING ESTABLISHED PLANTS

It is especially important to check climbers growing on house or garage walls as they can quickly grow into gutters, eaves and even roof spaces, where they can cause damage.

As hard pruning may delay flowering, lightly trim some shoots and cut back others hard, to ensure earlier flowering in the year, and even extend the flowering period; this works well with clematis, for example.

However, even fairly mild, regular pruning to tidy up an unruly climber – carried out too often and at the wrong time of year – will often result in little or no flowers as this can remove dormant

Walls create a rain shadow, where no rain will fall, so the soil can become very dry. To overcome this, plant about 45cm (18in) away from the base of a wall. Use a short stake or bamboo cane to guide the growth towards the support, in order to bridge the gap between soil and wall. This can be removed once the plant is established on the support.

Freestanding supports, such as trellis, frames or arches, do not create the same degree of rain shadow so the planting distance can be much shorter – anything from 15–30cm (6–12in). Use a short length of bamboo cane to help provide an initial growth guide until the climber has established itself on the permanent support structure.

flower buds. A vigorous climber that has been hard pruned of its 'bird's nest' tangle of stems may not flower for a few years.

• CLEMATIS •

Clematis is one of the most popular and versatile climbers. It is best pruned annually, although this is not essential, especially for the spring-flowering species and cultivars.

INITIAL TRAINING & PRUNING

Pruning at the time of planting will encourage bushier growth. Depending on type and timing, you may miss some flowers in the first year, but it is worth it.

Make sure that all resulting regrowth is trained to cover the support – preferably in a fan, or spiral pattern for a clematis growing up a post or pillar.

PRUNING ESTABLISHED PLANTS

An established clematis should cover its allotted space and produce plenty of leafy stems and flowers that can be appreciated at a suitable height. If left, clematis develops into a tangled mass, producing its flowers high up on leafless stems.

The time and amount of pruning needed by established plants depends on when each plant flowers. As a result, clematis are divided into three groups.

Group 1

This consists of clematis that flower in winter or spring on growth that was

---

FORMATIVE PRUNING A CLEMATIS

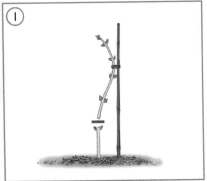

①

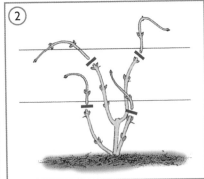

②

FIRST YEAR
In mid- to late winter, cut back the main stems of newly planted clematis to just above the lowest pair of strong, healthy buds.

SECOND YEAR
In mid- to late winter, shorten all main stems formed the previous year by about half to a pair of strong buds.

PRUNING ESTABLISHED CLEMATIS

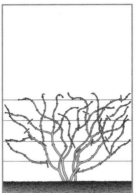

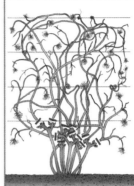

Group 1 clematis: After flowering, tidy up and prune to shape. Trim overlong stems and remove unwanted growth.

Group 2 clematis: In late winter, prune back to an established main framework. Cut back a few of the oldest stems to their base.

Group 3 clematis: In late winter, hard prune back to just above a pair of strong, healthy buds growing 15–30cm (6–12in) above soil level.

formed the previous year, and includes *C. alpina*, *C. armandii*, *C. cirrhosa*, *C. macropetala* and *C. montana*. Annual pruning is not essential for Group 1 plants, but they benefit from being tidied up and having any unwanted growth removed after flowering.

Group 2

In this clematis group are the hybrids that start to produce their flowers during late spring and early summer on growth produced the previous year. They also tend to produce flowers in late summer and autumn on the current year's growth. Again, it is not essential to prune group 2 annually, but they do benefit from a trim in late winter.

Group 3

This contains the clematis that start to flower from midsummer onwards, on growth produced that year. It includes *C. orientalis*, *C. tangutica*, the *C. viticella* and *C. texensis* varieties together with numerous large-flowered hybrids. All require hard pruning annually, in late winter, to keep them flowering well.

• WISTERIA •

Wisteria is an extremely versatile climber, which can be trained against a wall or be grown over a pergola or arch, where its blooms can be appreciated cascading overhead. Whichever way you train it, you will need to prune it correctly if you want a spectacular display of flowers.

The extension growth of these vigorous climbers can reach 3–3.7m (10–12ft) every year and can soon get out of control. When grown on a house wall, wisterias can easily invade gutters and downpipes and even damage roof tiles.

ESPALIERS

To cover a wall or fence, a wisteria looks much better if it is trained as an espalier with horizontal branches forming the main framework of the plant.

Spend the first few years training the main stems so they develop a strong framework of branches that fully cover the support.

ESTABLISHED ESPALIERS

Once the basic framework of espalier branches has been formed to fill the required space, you can then prune for flowers. This needs to be done twice a year – in summer, about two months after flowering, and again during winter (see p92).

Train wisteria initially to build up a framework, and then prune it to encourage flowers.

FORMATIVE PRUNING A WISTERIA ESPALIER

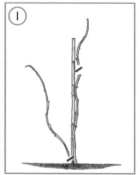

FIRST YEAR
After planting in winter, prune the strongest main stem to a bud 75–90cm (2½–3ft) above ground level. Carefully tie it to a vertical stake attached to the support wires. Cut back all other shoots to their base and remove any sideshoots on the main stem.

In summer, tie in the main shoot vertically as it grows. Select the two strongest sideshoots, one on each side, and train them at 45 degrees. Trim any secondary shoots on these sideshoots to 15cm (6in). Remove any growth from the base and other sideshoots.

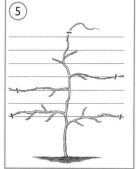

SECOND YEAR
In winter, cut back the main shoot to 75–90cm (2½–3ft) above the top sideshoot. Untie the two main sideshoots that were at 45 degrees and cut them back by about one third. Then carefully lower them and tie them in horizontally to the support wires.

Continue to train the main shoot vertically and tie in to the supports. As in step 2, in summer, choose another pairs of sideshoots and tie them in at 45 degrees, and trim secondary shoots. Remove other sideshoots and growth at the base. Trim sideshoots so they fit the allotted space.

THIRD & SUBSEQUENT YEARS
In winter, cut back the main shoot to 75–90cm (2½–3ft) above the new set of upper sideshoots. Untie the upper sideshoots and shorten them, and the others, back by about one third. Carefully lower the upper sideshoots and tie them in horizontally to the support wires.

In summer, shorten the extension growth and any lateral growth, to keep them under control as well as to build up short flowering spurs, on which the flowers are produced the following year. At the same time, choose shoots to tie in to the support to help improve coverage of the support. Cut out branches that are past their best or have become damaged and tie in their replacements.

In winter, it is easy to distinguish the plumper flower buds from the smaller, flattened growth buds when shortening any regrowth on the laterals or sideshoots.

OTHER METHODS OF TRAINING

Even plants that are grown more informally will benefit from regular summer and winter pruning to encourage flowering.

Where space is at a premium, wisteria can be grown in a more restricted growth form – this includes training it up a post, over a pergola and even as a standard (see p55).

After planting a wisteria against a post or pergola, initial training involves carefully winding the stems around the vertical posts as they develop, because this restricts their growth and

92

PRUNING AN ESTABLISHED WISTERIA ESPALIER

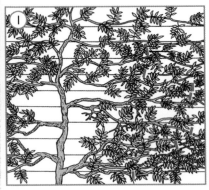

In midsummer, shorten all the long, whippy extension growth back to 5–7 leaves (approximately 15cm/6in) from where they join the main framework of the wisteria.

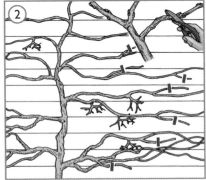

In midwinter, further cut back all the extension growth that was pruned in summer to short spurs, 2.5–5cm (1–2in) long, bearing 2–3 buds.

Wisteria can produce massed floral displays of beautifully scented flowers.

encourages flowering. As they elongate, tie in the stems regularly to the supports, using string in a figure of eight.

In these cases, it is usually better to prune more often, even though this is more laborious and requires regular attention. Therefore, every two weeks in summer, cut back the extension growth to 15–30cm (6–12in). This stimulates further laterals to form and constant pinching back produces more congested flowering spurs and so more flowers, which may be an important feature in smaller spaces.

PRUNING NEGLECTED WISTERIA

Because wisterias produce lots of long, whippy stems, if they are not pruned regularly the plants soon get out of control and the flowers are hidden in the mass of foliage. For plants that have been badly neglected and therefore need renovating, pruning is best carried out over several years.

In winter, remove all damaged, old or unwanted branches by cutting them back to a suitable branch or prune them out completely at their base. Cut off long branches in sections to prevent damage to other branches as well as making them easier to remove (see p66). Tie in replacement branches so they completely cover the support.

After pruning, make sure you feed the plant well with a balanced, granular fertiliser to aid swift recovery and healthy regrowth.

Such hard renovation pruning of a wisteria is likely to reduce flowering for the first few years.

· HONEYSUCKLE ·

Honeysuckles are popular twining climbers, but if left to their own devices they soon become an entangled mess of stems that not only looks unsightly but can also be very difficult to train and prune to shape. Neglected plants will have numerous leafless, bare stems at their base and produce few flowers.

After planting, therefore, always do some initial training and formative pruning. Then, in subsequent years, prune to keep plants compact and in good shape to cover their supports better and to encourage flowering.

Honeysuckles are split into two groups for pruning purposes, depending on their flowering habit.

GROUP 1

The first group includes vigorous evergreen honeysuckles, such as *Lonicera henryi*, *L. hildebrandiana* and *L. japonica*. They produce their flowers in summer and autumn on the current year's growth. They do not need regular pruning for flower production, but as they are quick growers their growth needs to be controlled.

In early spring, cut back overlong stems, thin out congested growth. Remove or cut back hard all weak, thin or damaged shoots.

Renovate very mature or neglected honeysuckles in winter by cutting all stems back to 60–90cm (2–3ft) above ground level. They will normally produce a mass of new stems after such hard pruning. This regrowth is likely

FORMATIVE PRUNING HONEYSUCKLE

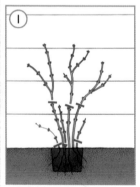

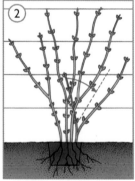

At planting time, cut back all stems by around half – or more for very thin stems – to encourage new, strong growth.

Train and tie in the new shoots as they grow so they evenly cover the support. If growth becomes too congested, prune this back hard during winter.

When correctly pruned, honeysuckles blend well with other seasonal plants.

L. × tellmanniana and *L. tragophylla*. Prune them immediately after flowering. Shorten all stems by around one third and remove all dead, damaged or diseased growth. Alternatively, leave these climbers to scramble over structures or up into trees, but in time they may become overgrown and an unsightly tangle of stems and need controlling. Do this in winter by hard pruning the stems in the same way as Group 1 honeysuckles.

to need thinning out by the removal of the weakest and thinnest stems.

GROUP 2

This contains the deciduous and some semievergreen honeysuckles that flower in summer on the previous year's growth: for example, common honeysuckle (*L. periclymenum*) and its popular varieties as well as *L. × americana*, *L. × brownii*, *L. sempervirens*,

PRUNING AN ESTABLISHED GROUP 2 HONEYSUCKLE

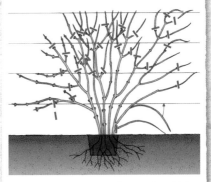

After flowering, shorten stems by around one third to tidy up the plant, encourage new growth to flower the following year and prevent plants becoming bare at their base.

· WALL SHRUBS ·

Some otherwise freestanding shrubs or those with lax stems can be trained as wall shrubs. These include bottlebrush (*Callistemon*), ceanothus, flowering quince (*Chaenomeles*), cotoneaster – especially *C. horizontalis*, pineapple broom (*Cytisus battandieri*), spindle tree (*Euonymus*), forsythia – especially *F. suspensa*, fremontodendron, silk tassel bush (*Garrya elliptica*), *Magnolia grandiflora* and firethorn (*Pyracantha*).

Also suitable are tender shrubs that like plenty of warmth and sun. Growing these against a south-facing wall is an excellent way of helping to ensure their winter survival, because the shelter and heat-absorbing properties of the wall provide extra protection against cold weather.

CEANOTHUS

These slightly tender shrubs are either spring-flowering, producing their flowers on the previous year's growth and are pruned after flowering, or are summer- and autumn-flowering, blooming on the current year's growth and pruned in midspring.

PRUNING A SPRING-FLOWERING CEANOTHUS

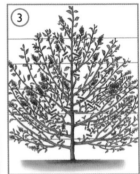

FIRST YEAR
In spring, tie in the main shoot vertically. Spread out the side branches evenly and remove any crossing and inward- or outward-facing branches.

SECOND YEAR
After flowering, cut back hard any branches growing well away from or towards the support. Tie in other shoots to fill in the plant's basic framework.

THIRD & SUBSEQUENT YEARS
After flowering, trim back all flowered shoots to 10–15cm (4–6in). Shorten any overly long branches by one third at the same time.

PRUNING AN ESTABLISHED FLOWERING QUINCE

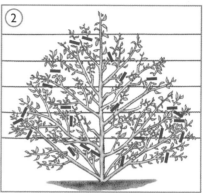

1 After flowering, shorten all flowered sideshoots by cutting back to 3–6 leaves. On well-established plants, cut back long extension growth unless it is needed for the plant's branch framework.

2 At the same time, remove badly positioned, dead, diseased, damaged or crossing branches as well as any that grow towards or away from the support. This maintains an open and healthy permanent framework.

PYRACANTHA

Prune pyracantha to enhance its colourful autumn and winter berries and its white flowers in early summer. The flowers are produced on the previous year's growth, so encourage these by following the pruning method for ceanothus (see left). After initial training, shorten extension growth in spring to retain the shape, even though some flowering growth will be removed. In late summer, shorten the extension growth to expose the developing berries.

FLOWERING QUINCE

Flowering quince makes a handsome wall shrub, flowering in spring on one-year-old and older growth. It also produces ornamental fruit. It can be trained as an espalier, like wisteria (see p90), or as a more informal wall shrub. For a multistemmed framework, retain several main stems.

CLIMBING HYDRANGEA

Although it is important to keep wall shrubs trained and pruned close to the wall, do not prune too close or you may remove flowering shoots. This is especially true for climbing hydrangea (*H. anomala* subsp. *petiolaris*), which produces its flowers on short stems that grow away from the plant and pruning these will prevent flowering.

HEDGES

• INTRODUCTION •

Hedges make natural barriers around or within gardens and can be a feature in their own right (for example, as parterres; see p55). When used as a screen or barrier, a hedge will give privacy and security or act as a windbreak, providing protection from cold winds, for example. It can be used to hide eyesores, such as ugly buildings, and to filter out noise. Most hedges will also provide food, shelter and nesting sites for wildlife.

In addition, hedges can be used throughout the garden to help break it up into smaller sections or 'rooms', and dwarf hedges can be introduced to edge paths, beds and borders. They do not have to be large and only grown around the perimeter of the garden.

A well-grown hedge should be thick and well clothed with foliage. Fortunately, there is a wide choice of hedging plants – just about any plant that can be pruned regularly is suitable.

TYPES OF HEDGE

There are two basic types of hedge – formal and informal.

Formal hedges have tightly clipped sides and are usually clothed to ground level with leaves, so plants need to have a dense habit and be tolerant of regular clipping. Many conifers, for example, make excellent formal hedges.

TYPES OF HEDGE

The shape and style of a hedge depends on its function. Formal hedges make excellent barriers or windbreaks and are often used to partition a garden. Informal hedges need less frequent clipping and can be very ornamental if made of flowering and fruiting shrubs.

Informal hedge

Formal hedge

HEDGING PLANT SELECTOR

Formal evergreen
Buxus (box)
Chamaecyparis
Cupressus
x *Cuprocyparis leylandii*
 (Leyland's cypress)
Elaeagnus
Escallonia
Euonymus
Griselinia
Ligustrum (privet)
Lonicera nitida
Myrtus communis
 (common myrtle)
Photinia
Prunus laurocerasus (laurel)
P. lusitanica (Portugal laurel)
Taxus (yew)
Thuja

Less formal evergreen
Aucuba (spotted laurel)
Choisya
Olearia (daisy bush)
Pittosporum
Rhododendron
Viburnum tinus

Formal deciduous
Acer campestre (field maple)
Carpinus betulus (hornbeam)
Fagus sylvatica (beech)

Informal deciduous flowering
Forsythia
Fuchsia
Potentilla
Prunux x *blireana, P. cerasifera*
Ribes (flowering currant)
Spiraea
Symphoricarpos (snowberry)

Dwarf hedge/edging
Buxus, dwarf varieties
Lavandula (lavender)
Podocarpus alpinus
Rosmarinus (rosemary)
Santolina
Rhododendron, dwarf varieties

Wildlife
Corylus (hazel)
Cotoneaster
Crataegus (hawthorn)
Prunus spinosa

Thorny security
Berberis
Hippophae
Ilex (holly)
Pyracantha (firethorn)
Rosa

Informal hedges are basically screens, and you can choose plants with colourful foliage, attractive flowers and/or autumn fruit for extra interest.

Select a plant that will grow to the size, type and style of hedge you want, such as: a formal evergreen hedge; an informal deciduous flowering hedge; a wildlife hedge; or a thorny security hedge (see box above).

TOOLS

Most hedges, especially those of conifers or plants with small leaves, are best pruned by trimming with hedging shears or a powered hedgetrimmer.

Carefully cut hedges with large leaves, such as laurel, with secateurs, loppers or saws; this avoids the ragged-cut edges that pruning with shears would produce and it minimises the risk of disease.

• FORMATIVE PRUNING
OF A DECIDUOUS HEDGE •

GETTING STARTED

A hedge is a long-term garden feature, so it needs to be planted correctly in well-prepared soil and cared for from the start. Ensuring that there is plenty of strong, healthy growth from the beginning will help the hedge to reach the desired height at the earliest opportunity and fill in its sides quickly.

The distance between plants will affect how quickly the hedge knits together, and depends on the vigour of the plant chosen; most are planted 38–60cm (15–24in) apart, whereas vigorous conifers such as Leyland cypress (× *Cuprocyparis leylandii*) can be planted 75–90cm (2½–3ft) apart.

After planting, tidy up unwanted growth and any shoots that are dead, dying, diseased or damaged.

Although, in the past, hedging plants were pruned hard after planting to

PRUNING A NATURALLY BUSHY, DECIDUOUS HEDGE

SECOND YEAR
Between autumn and late winter, trim back the main stem and side branches by one third. Cut to a healthy bud (see inset).

THIRD & FOURTH YEAR
Between autumn and late winter, shorten all new growth by about one third. The hedge will start to thicken up.

SUBSEQUENT YEARS
In early summer and again in winter, shorten the sides. Cut back to a permanent framework with well-tapered sides.

*Regular trimming will keep
a deciduous hedge bushy
and well clothed in foliage
for much of the year.*

stimulate bushy growth, it has been shown that this is unnecessary. Leave the first major pruning until the second growing season after planting.

Make sure the hedging plants are watered well during dry periods in spring and summer, as there will be a lot of competition at the roots for moisture and nutrients. Also feed them in spring and mulch with a thick layer of organic matter every year.

When pruning, always cut with a pair of good-quality, sharp secateurs; use loppers for larger branches. Make slanting cuts, just above a bud, angling each one away from the bud (see p20).

NATURALLY BUSHY HABITS

In the second growing season after planting, lightly prune the leader shoots of hedging plants that are naturally bushy at their base, such as beech (*Fagus*) and hazel (*Corylus*) and flowering shrubs such as forsythia. At the same time, shorten some of the longer side branches. This should be repeated in the third and fourth years.

To even up unbalanced growth, always prune strong shoots lightly and weak ones hard. Thus, you should shorten very vigorous leaders and side branches by no more than one third, while the weaker ones can be cut back by up to two thirds of their length.

NATURALLY ERECT HABITS

Hard prune vigorous plants with a more upright habit, such as hawthorn (*Crataegus*), to encourage strong, bushy growth. In summer, cut back the side branches and, in the second winter, prune hard again to remove about half of the previous year's growth.

• FORMATIVE PRUNING
OF AN EVERGREEN HEDGE •

Initially, plant and care for an evergreen hedge in the same way as for a deciduous hedge (see Getting started, p102).

Thereafter, formative prune most evergreens minimally, by shortening very overlong side branches to maintain the shape of the hedge. However, a badly shaped or thin, leggy plant may need severe pruning to encourage it to produce stronger growth near its base.

Subsequent regular shaping of the sides of the plants will ensure they start to produce strong, bushy growth that will develop into a dense hedge or barrier. Prune the main upright shoots only when they have reached the desired final height for the hedge.

Wherever possible, cut back large stems to within the foliage canopy, so that the growth hides the cut ends.

PRUNING AN EVERGREEN HEDGE

SECOND YEAR
In spring, cut evergreens by around one third. Only hard prune the plant if growth is weak or leggy.

THIRD & FOURTH YEARS
In summer, lightly trim back side branches. The following early spring, prune harder to start forming a shape with tapered sides.

SUBSEQUENT YEARS
Allow the hedge to fill out to its full size, continuing to trim twice a year to maintain the tapered shape.

• FORMATIVE PRUNING
OF A CONIFER HEDGE •

After planting, trim any untidy side branches to keep them in check and to encourage sideways growth that will fill in the hedge. In subsequent years, trim the sides to achieve the desired shape.

When training a conifer hedge, allow the plants to grow up to 15cm (6in) beyond the desired height before pruning the main upright stems, at which point you should remove the top 30cm (12in) of growth from the main stems. That way you will hide the unsightly cut ends of the main stems, which will otherwise stick out above the top of the hedge.

Once formed, most conifer hedges need cutting once or twice in summer to maintain their shape and bushy growth.

Prune fast-growing Leyland cypress more often, to keep it in control. Trim it regularly between late spring and late summer, to prevent wind and cold weather causing the cuts to turn brown and spoiling its overall look.

PRUNING A CONIFER HEDGE

SECOND YEAR
In winter, prune the side branches by about one third (see inset). Continue to tie the unpruned leading shoot to a stake as it grows.

THIRD & FOURTH YEARS
In summer, trim back sideshoots, gradually aiming to form the tapered shape. Continue tying in the leading shoot.

SUBSEQUENT YEARS
In summer, trim to maintain the tapered shape. Prune the leading shoot when the hedge has reached the required height.

• PRUNING ESTABLISHED HEDGES •

INFORMAL HEDGES

The timing and techniques used for pruning established informal hedges are more or less the same as for the relevant freestanding specimen (see Plant directory, p162). However, in addition to general pruning such as removing dead, damaged, diseased or unwanted growth and trimming back to keep the plants within bounds, hedge cutting also involves shaping the hedge to produce a solid, but natural looking outline. Take extra care with your timing and pruning cuts if you are trimming a hedge grown especially for its flowers or fruit, to ensure there is a display the following year.

FORMAL HEDGES

Established formal hedges need regular and correct pruning to ensure they maintain their shape, produce dense growth with a neat outline and do not start to develop bare areas or patches, especially at their base. This may mean cutting them at regular intervals throughout summer.

The aim with a formal hedge is to achieve a tapered outline with the base wider than the top, that is a hedge with a flat-topped or round-topped 'A'. The sides should slope slightly inwards from the base, so that light can reach the lower part of the hedge. If the hedge has straight sides or sides that taper inwards

VARIATIONS IN HEDGE BASE THICKNESS

Hedges with no initial pruning tend to grow upwards quickly, forming branches at the top at the expense of lower ones, resulting in bare bases.

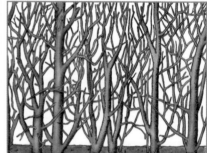

Hedges that are correctly pruned when young form dense growth that is evenly distributed from top to bottom. Such hedges look much better.

Hedges are not only good for creating boundaries but they are also useful ornamental features when properly looked after.

from the top, the lower part of the hedge will be shaded, and produce a bare, or straggly, bottom.

Hedges that are wider at the top are also prone to snow loading, the upper, outer branches become weighed down and bend or, in some cases, snap. This will cause the hedge to become untidy or even damaged.

Dwarf hedges and edging do not need to be tapered and look better with vertical sides.

The easiest way to produce a flat-topped 'A'-shaped hedge is to cut to a straight edge or use a garden line stretched between upright supports. To produce an even, round-topped hedge

you may want to create a wooden or hardboard template cut to the required shape. Place the template over the hedge and use it as a guide when cutting; move it along as you progress along the hedge.

Always check for nesting birds before you start cutting a hedge and ensure fledglings have flown the coop first.

Most formal hedges are trimmed twice a year; deciduous hedges when they are dormant in winter and again in midsummer; evergreens in late spring and late summer, although yew (*Taxus*) needs cutting only in summer and Leyland cypress may need three cuts – a final cut during late summer should deter excessive regrowth in autumn.

If not pruned regularly, hedges can soon get out of control. In such situations, hard renovation pruning may be the best way of getting the hedge back into shape and height.

Many hedges respond well to renovation pruning: for example, beech, hawthorn, holly (*Ilex*), hornbeam (*Carpinus*), *Lonicera nitida* and privet (*Ligustrum*). Apart from yew, conifer hedges do not reshoot well or at all from old wood, so you should cut back them by a maximum of one third of the overall hedge height. Replace all hedges that do not tolerate hard pruning.

Those hedges that do respond well to severe pruning can be reduced by up to 50 percent in height and width, but because hard pruning removes many growth buds such pruning is best carried out in stages. If reducing both the height and width of the hedge, cut back the top and one side in the first year, and shorten the other side the following year. If recovery is poor, delay the second cut for another 12 months.

Feed the hedge well the season prior to renovation and feed, water and mulch the soil after renovation to help aid a swift recovery.

Deciduous hedges are best renovated in midwinter, evergreens in midspring and conifers in spring.

To ensure a dense, even surface to a rejuvenated hedge, shorten stems by 15–20cm (6–8in) more than the required final height and spread, so the new growth can grow beyond, and hide, the cut ends.

If a hedge contains individual dead areas, it may be possible to train and tie in nearby living stems to cover them.

RENOVATING A HEDGE

Cut back hard one side of the hedge. If regrowth has been good, repeat on the other side the following year. If not, wait a further 12 months.

OVERTALL HEDGES

Legislation empowers people whose gardens are overshadowed by tall hedges to have the opportunity to resolve the problem without involving lawyers.

The Anti-Social Behaviour Act 2003: Part 8 states that people whose 'reasonable' enjoyment of their property is impaired by high hedges in close proximity can have the effects alleviated. For the purposes of this law a hedge is two or more trees in a line.

Enforcement of hedge height reduction is limited to what is sufficient for those affected to enjoy reasonable

When renovating a hedge, ensure that it will create interest, structure and focal points within the garden.

use of their property, rather than a specified height.

If overtall hedges affect your garden, contact your local council or the Department for Communities and Local Government for guidance. The latter has produced some booklets on how to complain and respond to complaints. These are available from the Communities and Local Government website – www.communities.gov.uk.

ROSES

• INTRODUCTION •

Because roses range from miniatures, which are often less than 30cm (12in) tall, to vigorous climbers and ramblers, which can easily reach 12m (40ft), a range of pruning techniques is needed to keep them within bounds, healthy and free flowering.

Pruning roses is as easy as any other group of flowering shrubs, and is not, as some gardeners would believe, difficult or complicated. For most rose plants, pruning does need to be carried out annually for best results.

PRUNING CUTS

Use sharp and clean secateurs or loppers to make clean cuts with no ragged edges,

to reduce the likelihood of disease. Make a 45-degree cut just above a healthy, outward-facing bud. Such a cut will help minimise die-back and rot in the bud. It will also induce new shoots to develop from the centre of the plant, thereby improving air circulation and reducing the risk of diseases, such as rose blackspot, by avoiding overcrowded shoots.

A pruning saw will be useful for cutting out very old and thick branches and will make a cleaner cut than loppers.

Although accurate pruning is usually recommended for roses, it is possible to prune with a hedgetrimmer if you have a lot of them. Research shows that this works for up to four years; after that it

GOOD AND BAD PRUNING CUTS

✓    ✗    ✗    ✗    ✗

Make a sloping cut 5mm (¼in) above a bud.   *Ragged cuts can lead to disease infection.*   *A cut made too high above a bud will cause die-back.*   *Cutting too close to a bud damages it.*   *A cut made towards the bud causes it to rot.*

is best to go back to pruning individual stems with secateurs.

BASIC STEPS

Start by cutting out all dead, dying, diseased and damaged stems to leave a framework of healthy branches to prune to. Always keep the overall shape of the plant in mind, and with bushy roses aim to create an open-centred or goblet-shaped plant. Remove stems that are rubbing and those that cross from one side of the plant to the other.

DEADHEADING

Removal of faded and dead flowers will prolong the flowering period of those varieties that are recurrent or repeat flowering. Roses that produce attractive hips in the autumn are best left alone to set their fruit.

Do not deadhead roses with attractive hips, otherwise the plants will not develop this welcome autumn feature.

Although, when deadheading, the recommendation used to be that rose stems should be shortened back to five or seven leaves below the flowers, this practice is no longer advised. It is now believed that the more leaves that are left on the plant, the more energy it can draw on to produce further flowers. Therefore, you should carefully snap off each dead rose flower at the abscission layer – that is, the slightly swollen section of stem just below the flower and the point where the faded flower naturally falls off. This encourages quicker recovery and more flowers over a shorter period.

DEADHEADING A ROSE

Roses are best deadheaded by carefully snapping off the dead roses using fingers and thumb, rather than pruning with secateurs.

ROSE SUCKERS

Most roses are grafted or budded onto a rootstock, in which case there is always the possibility of suckers being produced. You will often read that it is possible to distinguish a rose variety from a sucker

because the sucker will produce leaves made of up of seven leaflets. However, this is not always the case. The best way of checking is to follow the stem back to where it originates; if it is above the graft union (where the cultivar joins the

Care for your roses and you will be rewarded with masses of flowers.

rootstock) it is from the cultivar and if it is below it is from the rootstock. Always tear off suckers – never cut them.

PRUNING A ROSE SUCKER

Standard roses are prone to suckering on their main stems, which may be part of the rootstock or another grafted species. As soon as you see a sucker, or another shoot, growing on the main stem carefully pull it off with a gloved hand. If you spot it early enough, you may be able to rub it out before it starts developing.

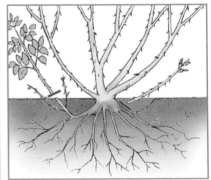

Remove suckers growing from the ground as soon as they appear. Carefully clear away the soil from around them and trace the sucker back to the main roots. Then rip it off at its base, which will remove any dormant buds. Never cut off suckers as this can leave behind dormant buds that can reshoot.

• ANNUAL PRUNING PROGRAMME •

The various types of roses require pruning at different times of year for optimum results.

Spring
Prune bush, shrub, miniature and standard roses in early spring. If severe weather is forecast, it is usually better to leave this task for a couple of weeks until the conditions improve or until growth buds begin to break. For bush and miniature roses, see p116; shrub roses, see p118; standard roses, see p120.

After pruning, give a generous feed with a granular rose fertiliser and mulch the soil around each plant.

Summer
Roses will be at their peak in summer, flowering profusely. Continually deadhead repeat-flowering or recurrent varieties to keep the flower show going for as long as possible,

In midsummer give a second feed of a granular rose fertiliser.

In late summer, cut flowering shoots off weeping standards (see p121).

Autumn
After flowering has finished for the year, cut back bush roses by up to half; shrub roses should be more lightly pruned. Such pruning has two benefits. First, it reduces the length of the rose stems, so the plants are less likely to be blown around in strong winds. Windrock can be transmitted down tall stems to the roots, moving them in the soil and damaging them. Second, it removes some of the growth in which pest eggs and the spores of diseases such as blackspot, rust and mildew can overwinter, ready to attack the plants again in spring.

After pruning in autumn, clear away all fallen growth, especially dead or dying leaves, to reduce disease problems.

Prune climbing and rambling roses in late autumn once all the flowers have faded (see p122).

From late autumn to midwinter, remove flowering shoots from weeping standards if not done in late summer.

Winter
If it was not carried out in autumn, prune climbing and rambling roses before midwinter.

In late winter, pruning of bush, miniature, shrub and standard roses can start if the weather is mild, instead of waiting for early spring.

Bush roses are the most popular type – mainly because of their very long flowering period, right through summer and autumn.

Roses planted when dormant can be pruned at the same time as they are planted. Those planted when in full growth should be tidied up at once, to remove dead, weak and spindly growth, and then pruned again the following winter or early spring.

HYBRID TEAS

Hybrid teas are sometimes referred to as large-flowered roses. Their main pruning is carried out in late winter or early spring, depending on weather conditions, but preferably before the growth buds start shooting. Remove all spindly growth, which is unlikely to flower and liable to succumb to disease. Shorten all remaining healthy stems back to 10–15cm (4–6in). Generally speaking, thinner stems need harder pruning to encourage new growth.

FLORIBUNDAS

The floribundas, which are usually more vigorous than hybrid tea roses, are sometimes known as cluster-flowered roses, because of their flowering habits. Their pruning is similar to hybrid teas, but should be less severe.

Shorten all the main, one-year-old stems by about one third, to within 23–30cm (9–12in) of ground level. Prune laterals or sideshoots back to two or three buds from the main stem. Cut back any older wood to within 15–23cm (6–9in) of ground level.

MINIATURE ROSES

The pruning of miniatures is similar to that for hybrid teas (see box right), although you should avoid cutting stems back too hard – especially after planting.

Remove weak and very spindly shoots and tip back stronger ones.

Hybrid tea roses bear large, individual blooms and need annual pruning.

PRUNING A HYBRID TEA BUSH ROSE

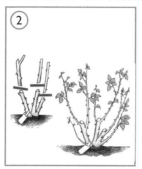

FIRST YEAR
If planting during the dormant season, prune roses before planting by lightly cutting back the main shoots, removing damaged shoots and pruning long, coarse or damaged roots.

In late winter or early spring, shorten each shoot back to 2–4 buds or 10–15cm (4–6in) above soil level (left). By summer, plenty of new shoots will have developed (right).

In summer, deadhead the plant. In autumn, trim back flowered stems to prevent windrock over winter. At the same time, cut out any soft, unripe shoots and congested growth.

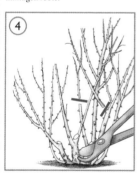

SECOND &
SUBSEQUENT YEARS
In late winter or early spring, cut out stems that are dead, diseased, damaged, crossing or growing inwards through the centre of the plant. Remove thin, spindly shoots.

Then prune strong stems, cutting them back to 4–6 buds or 10–15cm (4–6in) above soil level. Cut back the less vigorous stems harder, to 2–4 buds. Mulch around the plant.

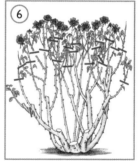

In autumn, once they have finished flowering, trim back all the flowered stems. At the same time, cut out any soft or unripe shoots as well as thin, spindly shoots.

Miniature rose plants sometimes produce overvigorous shoots, which can spoil the shape of the plant, and these should be cut back hard or removed right back to the source, to prevent them reappearing the following season.

These are the 'old' roses, and include the species roses as well as the albas, bourbons, damasks and gallicas among others. Most flower just once in summer, although some, such as the more modern New English roses, do repeat flower and may bloom freely for many years with little or no regular pruning.

When planting shrub roses from autumn to spring, also prune out dead, damaged or weak growth, and lightly tip back strong stems.

Shrub roses generally flower on older-wood and should be allowed to develop naturally, maintained by light but regular pruning and with a balance of older and young, vigorous growth.

Nearly all shrub roses usually flower well with minimal annual pruning.

However, there is a huge diversity among this group. Those with an arching habit, for example, need plenty of space; just shortening the stems to restrict their spread would spoil their graceful shape.

SINGLE-FLOWERING SHRUB ROSES

In late winter or early spring, cut out dead, dying, diseased and damaged wood, crossing or rubbing branches and thin, spindly growth. Prune the main stems lightly. Avoid the excessive build-up of older, unproductive wood crowding the centre. If the plants become leggy and bare at the base, remove one or two stems, back to near ground level, to encourage new, strong growth.

REPEAT-FLOWERING SHRUBS

Try to maintain a well-balanced framework of branches by reducing strong, new basal growth by up to one third and shorten strong sideshoots to two or three buds, from late winter to early spring.

Once the plants are mature, remove some of the older main stems back to their base; this severe pruning encourages vigorous, new shoots that will flower the following summer.

PRUNING A REPEAT-FLOWERING SHRUB ROSE

SECOND YEAR
In early spring, cut back the main stems by about one third and sideshoots by up to half. Remove badly placed and overcrowded stems back to their base.

Flowering begins on the pruned sideshoots in early summer. Repeat-flowering shrub roses will continue to flower throughout summer.

In autumn or early winter, if necessary, cut back the tips of very tall stems to maintain shape and minimise windrock, which loosens the roots.

THIRD & SUBSEQUENT YEARS
In early spring, cut back main stems by up to one third and sideshoots by up to one half. Remove up to three of the oldest stems at their base.

Flowering begins again in early summer, but more abundantly as there are now more sideshoots on which the flowers are produced.

In autumn or early winter, if necessary, cut back the tips of very tall stems. The aim from now on is to maintain a balanced, open framework to the plant.

119

GROUNDCOVER ROSES

These roses are very useful for growing over relatively large areas of ground. They need very little pruning, apart from removing wayward growth, to keep them under control. In late winter or early spring, tip prune stems to encourage bushiness and shorten any upright stems or those that extend over their allotted space.

• STANDARD ROSES •

Standard roses have a named rose variety (the scion) budded onto the top of a single, vertical rose stem (usually of *Rosa rugosa* or *R. laxa*), around 1.2m (4ft) above ground level, to produce a small rose 'tree' with a rounded flowering head. The scion varieties are usually a hybrid tea or floribunda. Shorter half-standards, quarter-standards and even patio standards are also available, and are more suitable for smaller gardens, growing in containers or where space is at a premium.

STAKING

The main stem of a rose standard is usually not strong enough to support itself, so the plant will need staking

PRUNING A STANDARD ROSE

FIRST YEAR
In early spring, shorten each stem back to 4–7 buds.

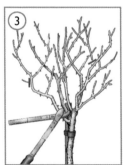

Throughout summer, deadhead spent blooms. In autumn, trim back the flowered stems to prevent windrock during winter. Also, cut out any soft, unripe shoots.

SECOND & SUBSEQUENT YEARS
In early spring, remove dead, diseased and damaged growth and any badly placed stems, to create an open centre.

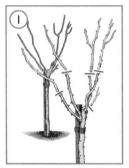

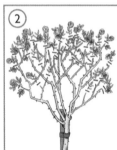

At the same time, shorten remaining branches back to seven buds. Cut back weaker stems to only 2–4 buds.

throughout its life. Use 2.5–3cm (¾–1in) square wooden posts and tie to the support with two rubber, tree or rose ties. Space these evenly along the standard stem.

PRUNING TECHNIQUE

To prune the head of a standard rose, follow the instructions for hybrid tea or floribunda roses, depending on which variety is used (see p116). But do not prune too often or too hard, otherwise suckers from the stem can dominate (see p114). Generally, stems can be pruned back so there remain four to seven buds from the bud union in the head.

As well as dealing with any suckers that develop from ground level, keep the main stem free from any side growth by cutting out or, better still, rubbing off any shoots as soon as they appear.

WEEPING STANDARDS

Weeping standards are similar to standard roses, except that a climbing or rambling rose scion is grafted on top of the rootstock stem. The stems then hang or weep down gracefully, rather than grow upwards (see box right).

Frequently, weeping standards are grown using a wire training frame (similar to an inverted hanging basket)

WEEPING STANDARDS

Prune weeping standards to keep excess growth under control and the centre of the head open. Do this once flowering is over or while the plant is dormant.

121

to which the stems are tied; this helps keep the head under control. This way any shoots, especially wayward ones, can be trained to fill in the head and ensure even growth, coverage and flowering.

To prune any weeping standard, remove the flowering shoots in late summer or from late autumn to midwinter. This will leave younger growth that will flower the following year. Cut back to an outward-facing bud or sideshoot to keep the centre of the head open. Then, if necessary, carefully bend down the shoots and tie them to the training frame so that they cover it evenly.

· CLIMBING & RAMBLING ROSES ·

Climbing roses are more compact than ramblers and so are the better choice for trellis, short lengths of fence or wall, posts and pillars. Ramblers are more vigorous, so need plenty of space and can even be trained into trees.

PRUNING A RAMBLING ROSE

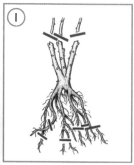

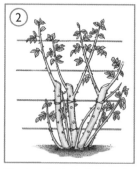

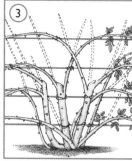

FIRST YEAR
Before planting, prune to leave 3–4 stems, 9–15cm (3½–6in) long. Trim long, coarse or damaged roots on bare-root plants.

New stems develop in the first spring and summer after planting to form the basic framework of the plant.

From early summer, train the stems onto the supports, to encourage new sideshoots to develop along the stems.

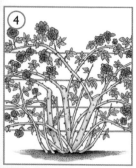

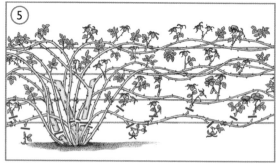

SECOND &
SUBSEQUENT YEARS
From early to midsummer, tie in stems horizontally as they develop. Flowers are produced on the previous year's sideshoots.

In late summer or early autumn, cut out a few of the oldest flowered stems to their base, leaving others to fill in the framework. Prune sideshoots to 2–3 buds, then tie in all the new stems to the support, keeping them horizontal to promote flowers.

Ramblers have lax habits and longer, more pliable stems than climbing roses, and they bear trusses of small flowers just once in summer. They also tend to produce more basal growth once they have become established. Climbers generally bear large flowers in smaller trusses on stiffer stems, and these can be produced in several flushes over a long period in summer and autumn.

SUPPORTS

Both climbing and rambling roses need suitable supports, such as stout trellis or a series of horizontal wires attached to a wall or fence, to which the shoots are tied. If using wires, place the lowest 45cm (18in) above ground level and space other wires 30cm (12in) apart.

If training plants up pillars, arches or pergolas, carefully bend the main shoots around the uprights to encourage flowering shoots to form low down.

PRUNING

Both climbing roses and ramblers can be successfully pruned at the same time of year, from late autumn to midwinter.

Their flowers are produced on a framework of mature stems and, to ensure plenty of flowers, it is important to train as many main stems as possible

horizontally (see p87). Therefore, in the first two or three years after planting, concentrate your formative pruning on developing the basic framework of main branches so they evenly cover the support structure.

Once established, the aim of pruning is to remove the oldest flowered stems and replace them with new ones, while maintaining the strong overall framework. This may involve completely cutting out one or two of the oldest stems if the rose has produced enough new growth since it was last pruned to replace it. This is usually the case with rambling roses.

Rambling roses are usually very vigorous and need plenty of room for growth.

· ROSE RENOVATION ·

Unpruned and neglected roses can flower without any attention for many years. However, eventually, they will start to become less vigorous, produce weaker stems and fewer flowers.

It is always worth trying to renovate such roses – even those that are 20–30 years old can be brought back to flowering life and a good shape. Very old roses that do not flower well and those that have not been pruned for many years may be better replaced.

Carry out renovation work in late autumn, winter or early spring, when the plants are dormant. It is best done over two – or more – years.

Shorten bush and shrub roses back to within 2.5–5cm (1–2in) of ground

RENOVATING A ROSE

FIRST YEAR
In early spring, cut out half of the oldest main stems to their base; leave the youngest and strongest stems. Shorten sideshoots back to 2–3 buds.

By midsummer flowers appear on the sideshoots of older stems. Vigorous, new shoots will grow from the base.

SECOND YEAR
In early spring, cut out the other half of the old stems. Shorten sideshoots back to 2–3 buds.

In early or midsummer, flowers are produced on the sideshoots. New, vigorous stems now replace the old framework.

124

Overgrown or neglected roses need renovation pruning to bring them back to shape and vigorous growth.

level. On climbing roses, cut back one in three stems to 30cm (12in) above ground level; repeat with the uncut stems over the following two years. On rambler roses completely remove old stems, leaving just three or four of the youngest, strongest stems. Then cut back any sideshoots to 7.5–10cm (3–4in).

Neglected roses often have very thick stems without any or many visible signs of growth buds. This is not necessarily a problem as adventitious buds often appear. On such plants, concentrate on making good, clean cuts – probably using a pruning saw on thick stems.

AFTERCARE

As always, follow up renovation pruning by giving each plant a good feed, using a granular rose fertiliser, to encourage new growth. Then apply a thick mulch of well-rotted manure around – but not touching – the stems.

A month after pruning, check the plant and examine its stems. If pruning has been successful, new buds will be emerging from the remaining stems.

Water regularly during dry periods in summer, to encourage the development of plenty of strong regrowth.

Continue to monitor the rose's progress throughout summer, and if regrowth is weak or poor apply one or two feeds of a liquid fertiliser one month apart to boost the plant.

Hard prune again in early spring the following year to remove the other old stems. If regrowth has been poor, remove only some of the oldest stems and continue with the pruning over a longer time. As before, feed and mulch plants, and ensure they are kept moist.

FRUIT TREES
& BUSHES

• FRUIT TREE INTRODUCTION •

The main fruit trees are apples, cherries, nectarines, peaches, pears and plums (including damsons and gages). For pruning purposes they can be divided into two groups: those that produce stones (cherries, nectarines, peaches and plums) and those that develop pips (apples and pears). These define the timing and, to some extent, the regularity of pruning. For example, stone fruit is susceptible to silver leaf and bacterial canker diseases, which tend to enter pruning cuts made in winter. Therefore, all pruning must be carried out after bud break in spring or in summer (see pp140, 144 and 146).

Apples and pears (see p130) can be pruned either when dormant in winter (which encourages leafy growth) or in summer (which encourages flowering and fruiting growth).

FRUIT TREE SHAPES

Different fruit tree shapes are suitable for different circumstances or habits of individual trees: for example, in a small garden a dwarf bush may be the best shape, or a cordon, espalier or fan trained along a wall or fence.

ROOTSTOCKS

A fruit tree comprises a scion (of your chosen fruit variety, e.g. 'Golden Delicious' apple) grafted onto a rootstock that not only controls growth rate but also affects when the tree comes into regular cropping. Thus the rootstock has a significant bearing on the training and pruning of a fruit tree. Always select the rootstock carefully, as growing a tree on too vigorous a rootstock may mean constant pruning back, consequently ruining its shape and cropping pattern. The vigour of the scion and the soil's fertility will influence the overall final height of the tree.

WIRE SUPPORTED
Cordon
This has a single stem with fruiting spurs. Double (U), triple (W) and quadruple (double-U) upright cordons are ornamental and produce good yields.

Suitable for: apples and pears and some soft fruit.

Espalier
In an espalier, pairs of opposite horizontal branches are trained off the main trunk, generally in three or four tiers.

Suitable for: apples and pears.

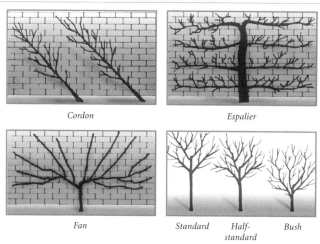

MAIN FRUIT TREE SHAPES

Cordon

Espalier

Fan

Standard   Half-standard   Bush

Fan

For this decorative shape a fan of branches originates from two main arms either side of a short main trunk. .

Suitable for: most tree fruit, but especially stone fruit.

FREESTANDING

Standard

These have a clear trunk of up to 2m (6½ft). The crown is formed in the same way as for a bush, but the height and spread are greater. Where space is limited, half-standards can be grown, with a clear trunk of 1–1.2m (3–4ft).

Suitable for: apple, cherry, pear, plum, damson, gage, nectarine, peach.

Bush

The bush fruit tree is the best size and shape for most average-sized or small gardens. The framework branches originate from a short main trunk, from 60–90cm (2–3ft) high.

Suitable for: apple, cherry, pear, plum, damson, gage, nectarine, peach.

Pyramid & dwarf pyramid

A pyramid tree is compact and reaches no more than 2.5–2.7m (8–9ft) high. It tapers upwards, so the lower branches receive sunlight to ripen the fruit. A dwarf pyramid is 1.5–1.8m (5–6ft) high.

Suitable for: apple, cherry, pear, plum, damson, gage.

FRUITING HABITS

Apple and pear varieties are divided into whether they are spur bearers or tip bearers, and this influences how they are pruned. Spur bearers produce fruit on short sideshoots, or spurs, along the branches of two-year-old wood. Tip bearers develop their fruit at or near the tips of shoots.

Most apples and pears are spur bearers. Tip bearers are best avoided when growing wire-supported forms (see p128), because of their pruning needs.

To prune spur bearers, you need to maintain a mixture of side branches at different stages of growth to be cut back after fruiting. This is achieved by spur pruning (see right) and renewal pruning (see p131). The latter is best reserved for the tree's outer branches where there is space for extra growth, while spur pruning is most useful for restricted forms and for building up fruit on freestanding trees.

For tip bearers, tip back the leaders of each main branch and the most vigorous laterals to the first strong bud. Leave unpruned any laterals less than 30cm (12in) long.

Pears tend to produce fruiting spurs readily, and these can become very congested if not thinned out in later years (see p138).

SPUR PRUNING

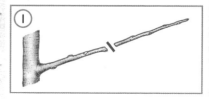

FIRST YEAR
From late autumn to late winter, select a proportion of new side branches that have insufficient space to extend into branches. Cut them back to four buds to encourage fruit bud formation.

SECOND YEAR
From late autumn to late winter, cut back each side branch to just above the topmost fat flower bud. If there is room for a bigger side branch, cut to four growth buds on last year's growth.

THIRD & SUBSEQUENT YEARS
A spur system will form, producing flowers and fruit. After several years, the spur will eventually become overcrowded or overlong and so need to be thinned in winter (see p138).

Once formative training has been completed and the main framework of branches formed, further pruning should concentrate on managing the fruit buds and the shoots they grow on, depending on whether the variety is a spur or tip bearer.

Ensure regular crops of pears by correct pruning as and when needed.

RENEWAL PRUNING

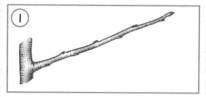

FIRST YEAR
From late autumn to late winter, select a strong, well-placed side branch and leave it unpruned.

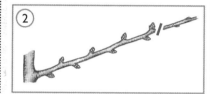

SECOND YEAR
Extension growth develops in summer and fruit buds form on the older wood. In winter, cut it back to the join between the old and new growth.

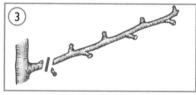

THIRD YEAR
Cut back the fruited stem in late autumn or winter to leave a short stub, about 3cm (1in) long, to encourage a replacement side branch to develop.

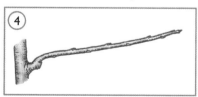

FOURTH & SUBSEQUENT YEARS
By the end of the growing season, a new vigorous shoot should have been produced. Leave this unpruned until the following winter, as in step 1.

STANDARDS, HALF-STANDARDS & BUSHES

Apples

There are several apple rootstocks available, so choose one suitable for the height of tree you want: M27, very dwarf, up to 1.8m (6ft); M9, dwarf, 1.8–3m (6–10ft); M26, semidwarf, 2.5–3.7m (8–12ft); MM106, semivigorous, 3.7–4.5m (12–15ft); MM111, vigorous, up to 6m (20ft).

Small bush trees are the best choice for a small garden, especially as two or more trees usually have to be grown to ensure successful cross-pollination. Always check whether the varieties you wish to grow are compatible for such purposes.

Most pruning of freestanding apple trees is carried out in winter when dormant, while wire-trained forms and dwarf pyramids are pruned in summer to help restrict growth and encourage fruiting. Remove surplus wood on established freestanding apple trees and encourage a steady supply of new shoots that bear fruit in later years. If left unpruned, growth becomes congested with older branches bearing fewer flowers and poor-quality fruit. Keep the centre of the tree open by removing larger branches; if several larger branches need removing then spread the work over two or three winters (see p148).

A well-grown apple tree will be productive and look very attractive, too.

132

PRUNING AN OPEN-CENTRED BUSH TREE

The technique is the same for half-standards or standards, except that the lowest branches start higher up on the main trunk.

FIRST YEAR
After planting a one-year-old tree, cut the main stem to a side branch. If there are no side branches, cut back the main stem to 75cm (30in), just above a bud. Make sure there are strong buds below the cut to form the new branches.

SECOND YEAR
In late autumn to early spring, choose four well-spaced branches to form the main permanent framework of the tree. Shorten them by half, or by two thirds if they are less vigorous. Prune to outward-facing buds. Remove unwanted branches.

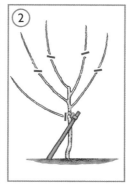

THIRD YEAR
In late autumn to early spring, select four more new branches and cut them back by half, or by two thirds if they are less vigorous. Prune them to outward-facing buds. Remove unwanted branches plus any very weak, dead or damaged growth.

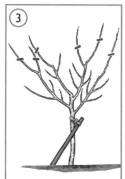

FOURTH & SUBSEQUENT YEARS
In winter, lightly prune the tree now it has reached cropping age. Keep an open centre by removing side branches on the inside of the tree, cutting back to 10cm (4in). Also remove any growth that is dead, diseased or crossing.

Pears

There are two main rootstocks for bush and standard pears: Quince C, dwarf, 2.5–3.7m (8–12ft); Quince A, semivigorous, 3.7–4.5m (12–15ft).

Pears grow in a similar way to apples but do, however, generally have a more upright growth habit and a marked natural tendency to develop spur systems. Prune them in the same way as apples, depending on whether they are tip-bearing cultivars or spur bearers. Thin out the fruiting spur systems before they become overcrowded (see p138).

DWARF PYRAMIDS

Dwarf pyramid trees were developed as a way of intensively growing fruit in a relatively small area as they can be planted quite close together. They are freestanding, but differ from bush and standards as they are grown as a restricted form.

The aim is to produce a tree around 1.5–1.8m (5–6ft) high with a spread of around 1.2m (4ft) at the base of the canopy, tapering to the top.

It is vital to keep such a compact and closely planted tree under control by summer pruning, completely removing vigorous, upright shoots and by growing on the correct rootstocks.

For apples, M26 and M9 rootstocks are ideal (see p132). For pears, choose Quince A or preferably Quince C depending on your natural soil fertility (see p133).

Spacing and supporting

Although one or two dwarf pyramid trees can

A pyramid tree is a suitable way of growing apples in a small space.

be grown freestanding, it may be better to support a row of trees by running two heavy-duty, horizontal wires between two stout posts. Secure the lower wire at a height of 45cm (18in) above ground level, and the second at 90cm (36in).

Space pyramids on M26 or Quince C rootstocks 1.2–1.5m (4–5ft) apart, those on M9 or Quince A 1.5–1.8m (5–6ft) apart. Use the wider spacings on fertile soils. When growing more than one row, set each row 2.1m (7ft) apart.

Established dwarf pyramids

When the tree has reached its final height of 1.5–1.8m (5–6ft), cut back

PRUNING A DWARF PYRAMID

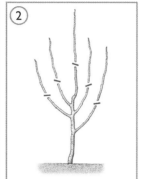

FIRST YEAR
After planting a one-year-old tree from autumn to early spring, cut back the central leader to just above a bud at around 50cm (20in) from ground level.

SECOND YEAR
From autumn to early spring, shorten new growth on the central leader back to 23cm (9in) just above a bud. Cut back new growth on the main branches to 20cm (8in).

In late summer, cut back to three leaves any side branch that is not needed for the tree framework. Shorten sideshoots to one leaf after the basal cluster.

135

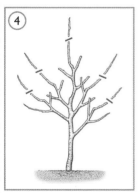

THIRD & FOURTH YEARS
In winter, cut the central leader to a bud opposite that made when pruning the previous winter. Prune the main branches, as in step 2.

In late summer, prune side branches and sideshoots, as in step 3. Cut back the tips of the main branches to 6–7 leaves.

In winter, prune the central leader, as in step 4 but on the opposite side. Shorten the main branches, as needed, to downward-facing buds.

the central leader almost back to old wood in late spring. Maintain the leader and retain the pyramid framework by pruning to shape and removing vigorous shoots. Thin sideshoots and prune spurs as necessary (see p130).

CORDONS

These consist of one or more single stems (see p128), each with many spurs; they are usually planted at a 45 degree angle, and tied to support wires. Several cordons can be grown in a small space.

On fertile soils, grow apples on M9 rootstock; on less fertile soils, use more vigorous rootstocks, such as M26 and MM106 (see p132). Quince C is the best pear rootstock for fertile soils; Quince A is better for poorer ones (see p133).

FORMATIVE PRUNING AN APPLE OR PEAR CORDON

FIRST YEAR
Plant a one-year-old tree from autumn to early spring and tie it to a bamboo cane secured at 45 degrees to the horizontal support wires. Cut back any side branches to three or four strong buds. Do not prune the leader.

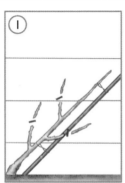

SECOND & SUBSEQUENT YEARS
Stubby shoots, fruiting spurs, should have formed on the previously pruned side branches. In spring of the second year, remove any flowers to stop the tree fruiting. In future years, retain the flowers, so they can develop into fruit.

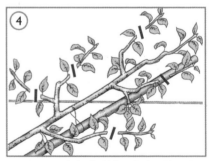

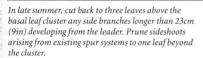

In late summer, cut back to three leaves above the basal leaf cluster any side branches longer than 23cm (9in) developing from the leader. Prune sideshoots arising from existing spur systems to one leaf beyond the cluster.

In autumn, just before leaf fall, cut back to old wood any new growth that develops from the pruned shoots. This will help build up further clusters of spurs that will flower, fruit and increase the overall yield.

PRUNING AN ESTABLISHED APPLE OR PEAR CORDON

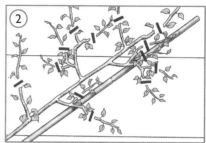

In late spring, cut back the new extension growth on the leader once it has developed beyond the top training wire and has reached the required height of around 2.1m (7ft).

In late summer, remove the new leading shoot that has grown in the place of the old one, cutting it back to 3cm (1in). Shorten to three leaves all mature side branches that are longer than 23cm (9in) and growing directly from the leader. Prune sideshoots from existing fruiting spurs to one leaf above the basal leaf cluster.

Partially trained one- or two-year-old cordon trees are available, and these will reduce the time taken to reach their full cropping potential.

Spacing & supporting

As cordons need very little space to grow in and produce a good crop, you can space them as little as 75–90cm (2½–3ft) apart in rows that run from north to south. If you require a second row, set it 1.8m (6ft) away from the first.

Secure the plants to three heavy-duty horizontal support wires 60cm (2ft) apart, held by strong posts or attached to walls or fence posts. Plant each cordon 15cm (6in) away from the support wires, angling the tree towards the wires.

Established cordons

Prune established cordons in summer when the basal third of new shoots have turned woody. Shorten side branches that are at least 23cm (9in) long back to the third leaf above the basal cluster of leaves. Shoots shorter than 23cm (9in) long are left unpruned. In warm climates, sideshoots that are 15–23cm (6–9in) long can be pruned.

Renovation

You can renovate well-established cordons in winter. Prune back the central stem by one third to promote extra side branches to form.

Winter is also a good time to thin out overcrowded spur systems (see p138).

ESPALIERS

There are several rootstocks available for espaliers. On fertile soils, apple espaliers can be grown on M26 rootstock; on less fertile soils or where you want a more vigorous espalier, use MM106 (see p132). Quince C is the best pear rootstock for fertile soils and Quince A is better for poorer soils (see p133).

Spacing & supporting

Space apple espaliers on M26 rootstocks 3–3.7m (10–12ft) apart and those on

THINNING OVERCROWDED
SPUR SYSTEMS

 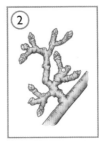

On older trees, spur systems can become congested, overlong or overlapping and need thinning out.

From late autumn to late winter, start by thinning out the weaker buds, then cut back some spur systems to two or three fruit buds.

MM106 3.7–4.5m (12–15ft) apart. Pears on Quince C are set 3–3.7m (10–12ft) apart and those on Quince A 3.7–4.5m (12–15ft) apart.

Fix the heavy-duty horizontal support wires 38–60cm (15–24in) apart – one for each tier of branches. For a partially trained tree, use the existing arms as the guide for the spacing between the wires. Plant 15cm (6in) away from the support wires, leaning the tree towards the wires.

Established espaliers

These are pruned in the same way as established cordons (see p137).

An espalier trained on a sheltered wall or fence should produce good crops.

PRUNING AN ESPALIER

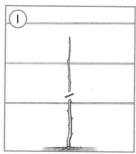

① FIRST YEAR
After planting a one-year-old tree from autumn to early spring, cut back the leader just above a bud at around 38cm (15in) from ground level. Ensure there are three good buds below this.

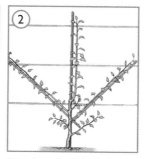

② Three shoots should develop. In summer, train the top shoot up a vertical cane secured to the horizontal support wires. Train the two lower shoots along canes at 45 degrees to the leader.

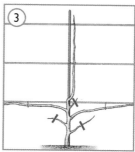

③ In late autumn or winter, lower the two side branches and carefully tie them to the horizontal support wires. Cut back to three buds any unwanted side branches on the leader.

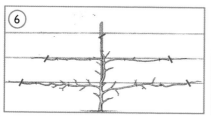

④ In winter, cut back the leader to just above the next wire, ensuring there are three good buds below this. If growth is weak, prune the side branches by up to one third to downward-facing buds.

⑤ SECOND & SUBSEQUENT YEARS
From summer to early autumn, train the second tier of side branches, as in step 2. Cut back to three leaves any sideshoots growing from the leader or the side branches.

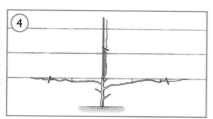

⑥ In winter, shorten the leader to just above the next wire, as in step 4. Tie down the second tier of side branches, as in step 3. Cut back the side branches by up to one third to downward-facing buds.

⑦ In late spring, when the espalier has filled its allotted space, cut back any new growth at the tips of branches to old wood. Afterwards maintain annually as for a cordon (see p137).

• PLUMS, DAMSONS & GAGES •

Plums, damsons and gages can be trained and grown as freestanding bushes, half-standards, standards, pyramids or as fans (see p129).

FREESTANDING TREES

For a small garden, Pixy dwarf rooting stock (to 3m/10ft high) is best for bushes, pyramids and fans when grown in fertile soil. St Julien A (to 4.5m/15ft) is semivigorous and so suitable for most soil types; it is ideal for bushes, half-standards and fans. For very vigorous, standard trees, choose Brompton rootstock (to 6m/20ft).

You can buy partially trained, two- or three-year-old bush, standard, half-standard and fan plum trees. Pyramid plums are best trained to shape from a one-year-old tree in your garden.

PRUNING A PYRAMID

FIRST YEAR
In midspring, shorten the leader to 1.2m (4ft). Remove all side branches lower than 45cm (18in) from the ground. Cut back the remaining side branches by about one half.

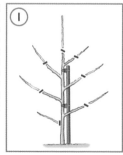

In midsummer, prune new growth on the side branches back to 20cm (8in) and shorten the sideshoots to 15cm (6in). Do not prune the leader – leave it to grow.

SECOND & SUBSEQUENT YEARS
In midspring, shorten the leader by up to two thirds of the previous year's growth. The aim is to keep the overall height of the tree to 2.5–2.7m (8–9ft).

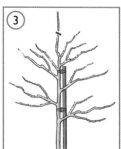

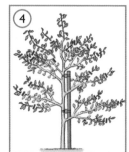

In midsummer, prune new growth on the side branches to eight leaves and the sideshoots to six leaves. Remove all vigorous shoots, especially those at the top.

Freestanding plum trees require only minimal pruning each year.

Pruning established trees

Plums fruit at the base of one-year-old shoots as well as along the length of older shoots. This means that the young growth does not need regular pruning, because the newest stems bear a good crop.

Pruning of most freestanding plum trees should therefore be kept to a minimum, although overcrowded branches may need removing, as well as weak, diseased, dying or dead ones.

Plums can produce a lot of fruit, which can cause the branches to bend and snap. To prevent this, thin fruit to 7.5–10cm (3–4in) apart. Otherwise propping up or supporting the branches may be required.

Renovate neglected plum trees over several years as they respond to larger pruning cuts by sending up masses of new shoots, which should be thinned to leave just one or two (see p149).

Formative pruning & training

Being a stone fruit, the main pruning of plums must be carried out when the plant is in growth, to prevent diseases.

In midspring, cut back the central stem of a one-year-old tree to a healthy bud 90cm (3ft) above ground level and shorten all side branches to 7.5cm (3in). In midsummer, select four or five of these and shorten the rest to four or five leaves. In the following spring, cut back by half the side branches left unpruned the previous year to an outward-facing bud. Remove all other side branches.

FANS

Most stone fruit needs a warm, sunny position to grow, flower and fruit well. Because of this they are best trained against a south-facing wall; the wall will absorb warmth from the sun and provide optimum growing conditions. Covering with fleece to protect the blossom from frost is also easier with wall-trained subjects.

Plums, gages and damsons generally flower early in the year, when pollination insects are scarce. It is, therefore, a good idea to hand pollinate the flowers with a soft brush to transfer pollen from one flower to another. Fans grown against a wall will start to flower earlier than freestanding trees, but if grown well and the growth is properly trained and pruned such fans are considerably easier to hand pollinate.

The fan is trained in position against the wall by pruning and tying its branches to heavy-duty, horizontal support wires secured to the surface usually 30cm (1ft) apart.

PRUNING A PLUM FAN

FIRST THREE YEARS
Formative prune, as for a peach fan (see p146), extending the framework to fill in the wall space. Prune any time the tree is in growth from midspring to late summer.

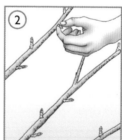

FOURTH & SUBSEQUENT YEARS
In spring, as growth begins, pinch out any shoots growing directly towards or away from the wall, using your thumb and forefinger. Leave only those that face in the direction of the fan.

From early to midsummer, pinch out the growing points of shoots not needed to create the framework, when they have six or seven leaves. This starts to build up the fruiting spurs.

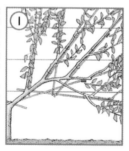

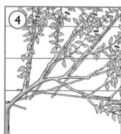

By late summer, cut back the pinched-out shoots to three leaves. This encourages the fruit buds to form at the bases of the pinched-out shoots during the following year.

Good crops of plums are easy to achieve when these trees are grown in a fan on a sunny, warm wall.

Formative pruning & training

Carry out pruning of these stone fruits after bud break in spring or in summer. The formative pruning of a fan-trained plum, damson or gage is the same as for a peach fan (see p146), but this changes as the tree becomes established.

Pruning established fans

The aim is to encourage fruit bud formation and, in later years, to replace old, worn-out branches. Do this by removing a proportion of the old wood, cutting back to young replacement branches from late spring to midsummer and training them in to the support wires.

Also, when pruning an established fan-trained plum, remove some of the older wood if there is a strong, young shoot lower down to fill in the gap. To help keep the fan's shape, cut back all new sideshoots to six leaves, with regrowth pinched out at one leaf. It is usually worth thinning out heavy crops to leave fruit 5–7.5cm (2–3in) apart.

After fruiting, shorten the pruned shoots again to one to three leaves. This allows the tree to direct its energies into next year's fruit buds.

143

• CHERRIES •

There are two main types of cherries – the sweet or dessert cherries and the acid or sour cherries. Unlike sweet cherries, acid cherries can be grown in a north-facing aspect. Both types can be trained as freestanding bushes, half-standards, standards or pyramids, but are more often grown as fans. Fan cherries have the same advantages as plums trained in this way (see p142).

The following rootstocks are available: Tabel, very dwarf, to 1.8m/6ft; Gisela 5, dwarf, 2.5–3m (8–10ft), Damil, semidwarf, 3–4.5m (10–15ft); Colt, semivigorous, 3.5–5m (11–16ft); Inmil, vigorous, 4.5–6m (15–20ft).

Plant freestanding trees on Gisela 5 2.5–3m (8–10ft) apart, while those on more vigorous roots, including Colt, need at least 4.5m (15ft) between plants. Even on Gisela 5 rootstock, each cherry fan requires plenty of space: allow 3.7m (12ft) wide by 2m (6½ft) of growing space.

You can buy partially trained, two- or three-year-old bushes, standards, half-standards and fan cherry trees, which saves training time.

Being a stone fruit, you should carry out the main pruning of a cherry tree when the plant is in growth.

SWEET CHERRIES

These plants produce fruit at the base of the previous year's growth and on older wood, unlike acid cherries, so they are pruned slightly differently. Prune a freestanding tree minimally; remove overcrowded branches if needed. For a fan, see right.

Grow your own cherries at home on freestanding or wall-trained trees.

FORMATIVE PRUNING OF A SWEET CHERRY FAN

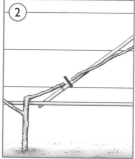

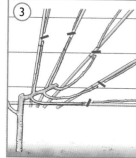

FIRST YEAR
In spring, tie two healthy side branches on opposite sides to canes supported on wires at 45 degrees. Cut back the central leader to the uppermost selected branch. Remove all other branches.

SECOND YEAR
In spring, shorten each side branch to 30cm (12in), cutting to a bud that points in the direction of the fan. This encourages stems to develop that will be used as the ribs of the fan.

THIRD YEAR
Tie in the sideshoots to canes supported on the wires. In spring, cut back all the sideshoots to suitable buds, leaving 45–55cm (18–22in) of new growth.

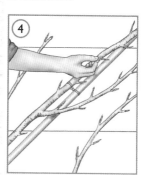

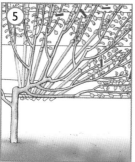

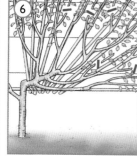

145

FOURTH & SUBSEQUENT YEARS
In spring, remove any new shoots that grow directly towards or away from the wall.

In midsummer, shorten to six leaves any sideshoots not needed for the framework. Cut stems that reach the top of the support to a stem just below or tie it down.

In late summer, shorten to three leaves the stems that were pruned in midsummer. This encourages fruit buds to form at the bases of the shoots for next year's fruit crop.

ACID CHERRIES

Acid cherries fruit only on shoots produced the previous year. On a freestanding tree, cut out some of the wood that has fruited each year as well as congested stems. For a fan, cut back each fruited stem to the replacement shoot at its base, after harvest.

• PEACHES & NECTARINES •

Peaches and nectarines can be grown as freestanding bushes, half-standards or standards, but are more often grown as fans. Training a peach as a fan has all the benefits as growing plums in this way (see p142). Peaches and nectarines are best grown on a south-facing wall and the flowers hand pollinated (see p142).

St Julien A is perfect for most gardens and soils, but you can use any plum rootstock (see p140). Partially trained trees are often available.

PRUNING A PEACH FAN

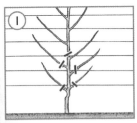

FIRST YEAR
After planting a one-year-old tree, cut back the leader to a side branch about 60cm (2ft) above ground level. Cut back other side branches to one bud.

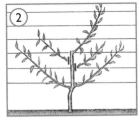

In early summer, select three side branches. Tie the topmost branch to the support wires and tie the lower branches to the left and right. Remove all other branches.

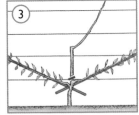

In early or midsummer, tie the lower side branches to canes set at 45 degrees. Later in summer, remove the central leader above the branches.

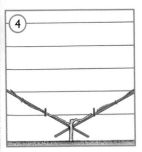

SECOND YEAR
In early spring, shorten the two side branches to a growth bud or a triple bud (a growth bud and two flower buds) at 30–45cm (12–18in) away from the main stem.

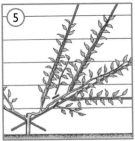

In summer, remove all but four sideshoots on each side branch to form the ribs of the fan. Tie them to canes attached to the support wires.

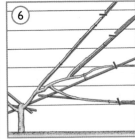

THIRD YEAR
In early spring, shorten by one third each sideshoot making up the ribs, cutting them back to a downward-facing growth bud.

As peaches and nectarines are stone fruit, prune them only in the growing season. They fruit on shoots produced the previous year. After fruiting, cut out the fruited stem (unless it is needed to fill a gap in the fan) and tie in its replacement. When pruning to produce a new shoot, cut to a pointed growth bud rather than a plump fruit one.

For formative pruning of a freestanding tree, prune as for an open-centred apple (see p133), but make all pruning cuts in spring or summer rather than in winter. For a fan, see below.

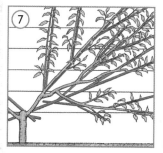

In the growing season, train three stems outwards from each of the ribs and tie them to canes. Leave other stems every 10cm (4in) and remove all the others.

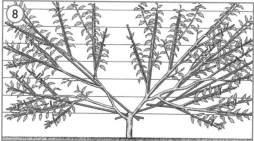

During the growing season, remove the growing point of each stem once it has made 45cm (18in) of growth, unless it is needed to extend the framework. This encourages the formation of fruit buds. In late summer, tie in the cut-back stems to canes on the support wires.

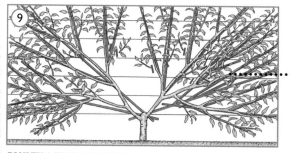

FOURTH & SUBSEQUENT YEARS
In late spring, prune to renew fruiting wood and maintain the framework. Remove stems growing directly towards or away from the wall. If any have rounded flower buds at their base, cut them back to one or two leaves.

· RENOVATING & RESTORING NEGLECTED FRUIT TREES ·

Fruit trees that have been neglected, badly pruned over several years or become stunted not only look misshapen but also produce poor, small and often diseased fruit. They may have also outgrown their allotted space.

STUNTED TREES

A tree can become stunted for a number of reasons: the ground around it may have become overgrown with weeds; it may have been planted in a lawn, which competes for moisture and nutrients; it may have been badly planted and failed to anchor itself properly in the soil; there may be insufficient light for good growth; and it may have been damaged by pests or diseases.

NEGLECTED TREES

Renovation of tall and overcrowded trees should be staged over several years because hard pruning results in strong, new growth at the expense of cropping. As well as removing unwanted and unnecessary stems, thin out spur systems that are overcongested (see p138) and remove weaker shoots where

RENOVATING A STUNTED TREE

 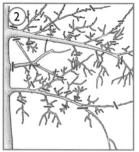 

In spring, remove grass and weeds from around the tree for a distance of 1.2m (4ft). Then mulch the soil. Drive in a stake and secure it to the tree with a tie.

In winter for pip fruit and in late spring or summer for stone fruit, thin out overcrowded fruiting spurs, if needed. Hard prune any young or weak growth.

In spring for one or two years, remove most or all of the fruitlets. Feed and mulch well in spring and control any pest or disease problems.

RESTORATIVE PRUNING AN OLD APPLE TREE

In winter, stand back and inspect the tree to assess the work that needs to be carried out. This tree has areas of congested growth, particularly around bad pruning cuts made 2–3 years previously, as well as low growth and some suckers.

Thin out congested strong shoots around wounds where branches were previously removed, cutting them out at the base. Do not prune out more than one third of such growth in one year. Remove crossing and other unwanted branches.

Aim to leave a healthy, evenly balanced framework of branches that are 60–90cm (2–3ft) apart. Over 2–3 years, continue to remove dead, crossing, rubbing branches and any congesting the centre of the tree.

In summer, a more balanced and open crown will develop that will produce strong and healthy, new growth that will fruit in future years. Resume normal pruning and maintenance once the renovation is complete.

possible. This should result in larger, better-quality fruit. Always feed, water and mulch the tree each year after such severe pruning.

Heavy pruning may result in water shoots (see p68). From these, select potential replacement branches; the final shoot spacing should ideally be at least 30cm (1ft) apart, so remove all other badly placed growth and thin overcrowded shoots.

Use very sharp loppers and saws for renovation work.

• SOFT FRUIT INTRODUCTION •

Soft fruit plants are generally much easier to look after than fruit trees. The aim of pruning is to keep the plants strong and healthy, so that they give large crops for many years.

Every garden should be able to accommodate at least a few plants, because soft fruit can be grown and, in some cases such as gooseberries and red and white currants, trained to take up very little space.

Soft fruit can be divided into three basic types: cane fruit; bush fruit; vine fruit. In addition there are strawberries, which are herbaceous plants that do not need pruning – apart from cutting off old or diseased leaves. Also, after cropping, remove all the old foliage by going over the plants with shears.

CANE FRUIT

Raspberries, blackberries and the numerous so-called hybrid berries are all cane fruits, which produce annual sturdy fruiting stems from ground level. They usually start to fruit in the second year after planting, but see primocane raspberries on p156.

Raspberries are very popular soft fruits and are easy to prune and train.

BUSH FRUIT

These include currants, gooseberries and blueberries. The aim of pruning is to produce a more-or-less permanent framework of branches. These may come from a single stem or leg (red and white currants and gooseberries) or they may be multistemmed (black currants and blueberries).

VINE FRUIT

Grapes are vine fruits. They are vigorous climbers that produce strong growth and need sturdy supports. When in fruit, their stems can become exceptionally heavy. They must be well trained and the growth restricted by regular pruning.

• BLACK CURRANTS •

Black currants are grown as stooled bushes, with its shoots growing from ground level. The best fruit crops appear on the previous year's growth, but they will also crop on older wood.

To create a stooled bush, plant it 2.5–5cm (1–2in) deeper than the plant had previously been growing, then shorten all shoots to 5cm (2in).

The aim of pruning black currants is to ensure the plant has a regular supply of vigorous branches from older wood.

For the first three years, if growth is strong prune lightly in winter to remove weak and low-lying growth. However, if growth is weak prune harder, cutting at least half the shoots to ground level.

Once established, cut out one third of the growth annually in winter, concentrating on old, unproductive wood and weak and low-growing stems to promote strong growth from or near ground level. Other fruited branches can be cut back to vigorous sideshoots.

PRUNING A BLACK CURRANT BUSH

FIRST YEAR
After planting from autumn to spring, cut down all shoots to within 5cm (2in) of the soil surface.

SECOND YEAR
In midsummer, the bush will produce its first fruits on one-year-old wood that was formed previous year.

THIRD YEAR
In late autumn, thin out weak shoots and remove low stems that have developed from the base of the bush.

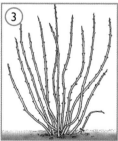

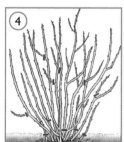

SUBSEQUENT YEARS
In winter, cut out about one third of the oldest stems and remove badly placed or damaged stems.

• GOOSEBERRIES, RED & WHITE CURRANTS •

OPEN-CENTRED BUSHES

Gooseberries produce their fruit on spurs on older wood and at the base of the previous year's growth. They are trained to form an open-centred bush, 1.2–1.8m (4–6ft) high, on a short stem or leg, with a strong framework of 8–12 main branches arising from the leg. Always remove any shoots developing on the leg.

The training of red and white currants is similar to that of gooseberries (see right), forming an open-centred bush on a short leg with 8–10 main branches. They produce fruit at the base of sideshoots formed the previous year. These are pruned in winter to produce short fruiting spurs that fruit annually.

After planting a red or white currant or gooseberry bush, cut back each main

Red currants are delicious summer soft fruit crops, but the bushes require careful pruning every year.

shoot by half to an outward-facing bud, or upward-facing one on a pendent stem, and remove any weak growth.

In the following winter, shorten these main shoots by half and select up to a further six strong shoots to form the other main branches and cut these back by half. Badly placed shoots and weak sideshoots are cut back to one bud, to encourage strong growth.

RENOVATION

Old, neglected bushes can be renovated by removing all the dead, damaged, dying and diseased stems and weak, crossing and rubbing branches, together with the unwanted main branches and then cutting back the sideshoots to one or two buds.

PRUNING A GOOSEBERRY, RED OR WHITE CURRANT BUSH

 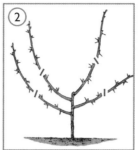 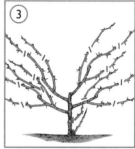

FIRST YEAR
Plant from late autumn to spring. In the first winter, remove any growth that develops from the main stem below 10–15cm (4–6in) above ground level, to maintain a clear stem, or leg.

Also in winter, cut back by one half the side branches that will form the framework, pruning to a bud that faces the centre of the bush and points upwards. This develops an open centre.

SECOND YEAR
In winter, shorten the branches by one third to half to inward- and upward-facing buds. Select well-placed sideshoots to form further permanent branches and remove low growth on the main stem.

153

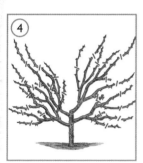  

THIRD YEAR
In winter, cut by half the branches to a bud facing in the required direction. Remove any shoots that are crowding the centre. Shorten any sideshoots not needed for the framework to 5–7.5cm (2–3in).

In late spring or early summer, thin gooseberry fruit by removing every other one; they can be used for cooking. Leave the rest to ripen and develop their full flavour and to their full size. Currants do not need thinning.

SUBSEQUENT YEARS
In midsummer, shorten to five leaves all sideshoots produced that year. Do not prune the main branches. Leave these until winter, cutting them back by half; also cut sideshoots pruned in summer to about two buds.

In subsequent years, cut back that year's growth to one bud in winter so that the bush has its main branches covered with short fruiting spurs. Old, unproductive and unhealthy growth can be removed, cutting it back to a strong, vigorous shoot. Also cut out any diseased, dying or damaged stems.

RESTRICTED FORMS

Where space is limited, gooseberries, red and white currants can be trained as restricted shapes, such as cordons, fans and standards. Lots of these plants will fit into a relatively small space, and they also provide an ornamental fruiting feature. As gooseberries, red and white currants tolerate shade, they can be grown against a north-facing wall or fence.

Cordons

Plant a single-stemmed young plant and tie it to taut, horizontal support wires, spaced 30cm (12in) apart.

In the first spring after planting, cut back the main stem by one half, and the side branches to one bud. In early summer, tie in extension growth on the main stem and shorten the new sideshoots to five leaves.

In the following winter, prune back the sideshoots to one or two buds. Shorten the main stem by one third of the new growth. Repeat these two steps every winter until the cordon has reached the required height.

When the plant is mature and established, stop the main stem at five leaves in early summer, and shorten the sideshoots to within one or two buds of the old growth in winter.

Fans

Plant a single-stemmed young plant and train it against a wall or fence, tying the stem to the heavy-duty, horizontal support wires, 30cm (12in) apart. After planting, cut back the stem to two strong sideshoots or buds about 15cm (6in) above ground level, which can be trained in opposite directions to form the main fan 'arms'. As these side branches grow, tie them to bamboo canes secured to the support wires at an angle of 45 degrees.

In the following winter, cut back both side branches by half and remove all other shoots. In summer, select three or four sideshoots on each of the two side branches to train as the main ribs of the fan. Remove vigorous surplus shoots, but retain any weaker ones, but shorten them to three or four leaves.

In the third winter after planting, prune back the shoots forming the ribs by one half and shorten their sideshoots to one bud. In summer, shorten all sideshoots to five leaves and then cut them again in winter to one or two buds.

In subsequent years, treat the fan as for an established cordon (see left).

When grown as ornamental, restricted forms, gooseberries will occupy only a little space in the garden.

There are two main types of raspberry varieties. The summer-fruiting ones, which produce fruit on the previous year's growth, and the autumn-fruiting ones, which fruit on the current year's growth. This difference affects how they are trained and pruned once established.

SUMMER-FRUITING RASPBERRIES

These are tied to three taut, horizontal support wires fixed at 75cm (30in), 1m (3ft) and 1.5m (5ft) above ground level and firmly anchored on sturdy posts positioned at the row ends.

After planting, shorten the stems in spring. The new canes that develop from the ground during summer will crop the following year. Prune them after fruiting (see page 157).

AUTUMN-FRUITING RASPBERRIES

These raspberries can be grown without supports, although in an exposed or windy site they do better with support.

They can be trained to grow between two sets of parallel wires set at 1m (3ft) and 1.5m (5ft) above ground level on supports 60cm (2ft) apart.

Like summer-fruiting varieties, cut back the canes to near ground level, after planting. The new canes grow from the ground during summer, and these go on to crop that year.

In late winter, before new growth starts, prune the fruited canes of autumn-fruiting raspberries down to ground level. As replacements, select up to eight of the best new canes per plant.

PRIMOCANE RASPBERRIES

Primocane, or long cane, raspberries have the advantage of fruiting in the first year after planting and of producing two crops per year thereafter on both the current and previous year's growth. After planting, unlike standard varieties, do not prune the stems down to ground level; these canes will produce the first year's fruit.

In subsequent years soon after they have finished cropping in autumn, select the stems that have just produced fruit at their tips and cut back these to a point just below where the raspberries were produced. These half-canes can then be left to overwinter. They will put on new top growth in spring and will then go on to produce the first crop of berries in early summer. After such two-year-old canes have finished fruiting, cut them right back to their base.

PRUNING SUMMER-FRUITING RASPBERRY CANES

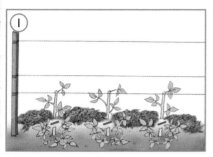

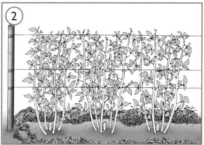

FIRST YEAR
After planting from autumn to early spring, cut down woody stems to ground level in spring. Leave the new canes alone.

In spring and summer, tie the new canes to the support wires as they develop. Keep the canes spaced about 10cm (4in) apart.

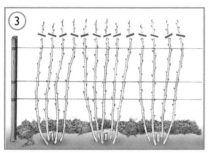

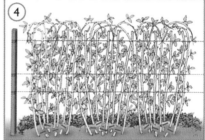

SECOND & SUBSEQUENT YEARS
In winter, cut back each cane to a bud 10–15cm (4–6in) above the wire if the canes have grown vigorously and are well above the top support wire.

In summer, cut the canes right down to ground level, after they have fruited. Tie in the new canes 10cm (4in) apart. You can loop overvigorous canes.

TRAINING AUTUMN-FRUITING RASPBERRY CANES

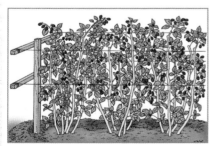

Autumn-fruiting raspberries fruit on canes produced during the current year. Unlike summer-flowering varieties, they do not need as much support and can be grown between parallel supporting wires. The canes do not require tying in unless the position is exposed to strong winds.

• BLACKBERRIES & HYBRID BERRIES •

Strict training and pruning are required to keep these very vigorous growers within bounds and make the fruit easier to pick, by separating the fruiting and new canes. They also need a sturdy support system of four taut horizontal wires, supported by sturdy posts, 30cm (12in) apart, the lowest 90cm (3ft) from soil level, the highest 1.8m (6ft).

There are four training systems.

Fan: In this compact system for less vigorous types, the fruiting canes are spread out on the support wires, and the new canes are tied together vertically in the middle of the plant.

Alternate: The fruiting canes are grown in one direction and new canes are trained in the opposite direction.

Rope: The fruiting canes are twisted together and tied along the lower three wires. The new canes are tied onto the top wire. When the fruited canes are cut out, the new ones are lowered to replace them.

Weaving: see illustrations below.

TRAINING BLACKBERRY CANES BY WEAVING THEM

FIRST YEAR
In summer, tie the young canes to the support wires as they grow. Train them vertically at first, then weave the extension growth in and out of the bottom three support wires.

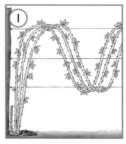

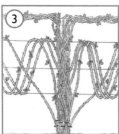

SECOND YEAR
In summer, train the new canes through the centre of the plant and along the top wire so that they do not interfere with the previous year's canes. The old canes will carry the current year's fruit.

In autumn, cut down all the fruited canes to ground level after fruiting. If there are not many new canes to carry next year's fruit, retain the best of the old canes to supply extra fruit.

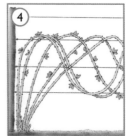

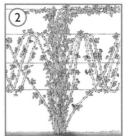

At the same time, untie the current year's canes and carefully weave them around the lower three wires and tie them in. In late winter, prune any damaged tips from the young canes.

• BLUEBERRIES •

The best blueberry fruit forms on short sideshoots produced during spring or early summer of the previous year. They can also develop a second, late flush of fruit on the tips of strong stems of the current year's growth.

Young plants need little or no pruning in the first three years. During this period, any cuts you make should be done between late autumn and late winter. Aim to produce an open centre by removing shoots that grow horizontally or are overly long.

On established blueberry plants, between late autumn and late winter, remove older stems lacking strength, thin out weak growth, crossing or horizontal shoots, as well as any dead or damaged growth. Cut back some branches to their base and others to strong, upright shoots. Prune stems that fruited the previous year to a low, strong-growing, upward-facing bud or shoot. By the end of pruning you should have cut out about 15 percent of the oldest growth.

Prune established plants by removing the oldest, least productive stems.

PRUNING BLUEBERRIES

Between late autumn and late winter, cut back fruited branches that have become thin and twiggy to a more vigorous shoot. Remove damaged and dead branches close to their base.

• GRAPEVINES •

Major grape pruning must be carried out in winter when plants are dormant, otherwise they bleed sap. However, cutting back soft annual growth and removing growing tips can be carried out safely in summer.

The vines will need to be secured to heavy-duty, horizontal support wires, usually spaced 30–40cm (12–16in) apart, with the lowest wire 40cm (16in) above ground level.

There are several training and pruning methods for grapevines, but the best for outdoor culture is the Guyot system.

GUYOT SYSTEM

This produces a short trunk with low, annually renewed, horizontal side branches and vertical cropping shoots.

After planting, cut back the main stem to about 15cm (6in) above ground level, leaving at least two or three good buds. Throughout summer, tie in the main stem vertically and remove any flowers that form.

Thereafter the aim is to create an annual framework of horizontal branches and vertical shoots on which the fruit forms. Once fruiting starts, from the third year onwards, thin bunches of grapes to 30cm (12in) apart.

CORDON OR ROD-&-SPUR SYSTEM

This is the best method for training indoor grapes.

After planting, cut the main stem to a strong bud just above the first wire. Cut back any side branches to two buds.

Throughout summer, tie in the main stem vertically as it extends, cut back side branches to five leaves and sideshoots on the side branches to two leaves. Remove any flowers.

In the second winter, cut back the main stem by about two thirds of the summer's growth to leave only ripened, brown wood, pruning to a healthy bud. Shorten side branches to one bud if they are strong, to two buds if not.

In the second summer, repeat the treatment of the first summer; and during the third winter, repeat the treatment of the second winter. Repeat the winter pruning in subsequent years until the main stem reaches the top wire; thereafter prune the main stem back to a bud at the top wire.

Each year, allow side branches to form at each support wire, left and right of the main stem; in summer, pinch surplus shoots back to one leaf. In winter, cut back all side branches to two buds.

PRUNING A GUYOT SYSTEM GRAPEVINE

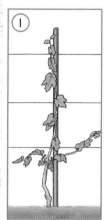 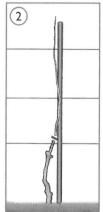 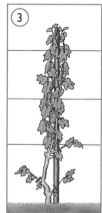 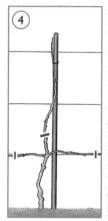

FIRST YEAR
Allow only one main stem to develop. Train it vertically up a cane tied to support wires. As they appear, pinch back any other stems to one leaf.

In early winter, cut down the main stem to around 40cm (16in) above ground level, ensuring that three good buds remain.

SECOND YEAR
Train the resulting three stems vertically throughout spring and summer. Also, pinch back any other shoots to one leaf.

In winter, tie the two side branches to the lowest horizontal support wire having shortened them to 60–75cm (24–30in). Prune the main stem to three good buds.

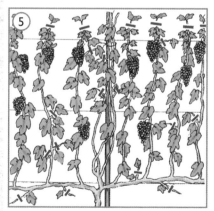 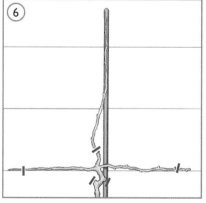

THIRD & SUBSEQUENT YEARS
On the main stem, train the three new shoots vertically. Allow several well-spaced, fruit-bearing shoots to grow vertically from the two side branches. In summer, cut back unwanted sideshoots to 3cm (1in) and fruiting shoots to three leaves above the top wire.

In winter, cut off both side branches. Shorten the two outer remaining stems to 60–75cm (24–30in), then tie them horizontally to the support wires. Prune the remaining vertical shoot to three good buds.

PRUNING
DIRECTORY

Plant name	Plant type	Pruning method
Abelia	Evergreen/ deciduous shrub	*Flowers on the previous year's growth and may also flower again later on the current year's growth. After flowering, remove up to one in four of the oldest flowered shoots, cutting back to strong, new shoots.*
Abutilon	Evergreen/ deciduous wall shrub	*Flowers on the current season's growth. In early to midspring, remove shoots that have been damaged by winter weather, any spindly, weak shoots and overcrowded shoots. A. megapotamicum and hybrids should also have old stems removed once a framework has been established.*
Acacia (mimosa, wattle)	Evergreen tree	*Prune plants after flowering to a strong sideshoot or 2–3 buds beyond the old flowers. Remove frost-damaged growth in late spring, but keep any other pruning to a minimum.*
Acer (maple)	Deciduous shrub/tree	*Maples should be pruned in winter when they are fully dormant, otherwise they bleed sap very heavily, which can weaken them. Very small cuts to remove thin shoots can usually be made in early spring, late summer or early autumn. Otherwise keep pruning to a minimum.* *A. japonicum, A. palmatum (Japanese maples) need minimal, if any, pruning and, in fact, prefer not to be pruned regularly.* *Tree species with attractive bark, such as A. davidii, A. griseum and A. pensylvanicum, are grown with clear trunks to show off the bark, so remove sideshoots and low branches up to at least 1.5–1.8m (5–6ft).*
Actinidia kolomikta	Deciduous climber	*Prune in late winter or early spring before new growth starts. Cut back young plants to buds 30–40cm (12–16in) above ground level to encourage bushy growth. In the following year, cut back strong sideshoots by two thirds, and weaker shoots to 1–2 buds. Once established, shorten stems by one third to one half.*
Aesculus (horse chestnut, buckeye)	Deciduous tree	*Keep pruning to a minimum; any pruning should be carried out from autumn to midwinter. Minor pruning to remove thin shoots can be carried out in summer.* *A. parviflora is a large, suckering shrub; if it becomes too thick, prune it in winter.*
Ailanthus (tree of heaven)	Deciduous tree	*Keep pruning to a minimum; any pruning should be carried out in spring. If the central leader is lost, thin out the resulting regrowth and allow the plant to develop as a multistemmed tree.*
Akebia quinata (chocolate vine)	Deciduous/ semievergreen climber	*Does not need routine pruning. Once established, it can be kept within bounds by pruning every few years after flowering. Prune the previous year's growth back by one half to two thirds.*
Alnus (alder)	Deciduous	*Established trees do not need regular pruning, except the removal of unwanted stems from autumn until midwinter. Minor cuts, to remove small shoots, can be carried out in summer.*

164

Plant name	Plant type	Pruning method
Amelanchier (snowy mespilus)	Deciduous shrub/ tree	*When growing as a multistemmed shrub, thin out one in three of the oldest stems in winter. To grow as a tree, select the straightest, strongest stem and remove all sideshoots to create a trunk 60cm–1.8m (2–6ft) long. Then allow a branched head to form, selecting and retaining sideshoots to create an evenly spaced framework of branches.*
Ampelopsis	Deciduous climber	*Pruning should be carried out in winter. Where space is restricted, train as many shoots as is needed, remove the rest and each year cut back all young shoots to within 2–3 buds of these main stems.*
Arbutus (strawberry tree)	Evergreen shrub	*Pruning of established plants is best kept to a minimum, although weak growth and dead branches should be removed. If grown as a tree, keep the central leading shoot and remove low sideshoots if necessary to display the main trunk.*
Artemisia (wormwood)	Evergreen/deciduous shrub	*Prune in early to midspring, after there is little risk of frost, to produce bushy growth and prevent the plant becoming bare and leggy at the base. Cut back all stems to 5cm (2in) from the ground in the first spring after planting. Thereafter, cut back the previous year's growth by up to one half each year and remove any growth damaged by winter weather.*
Aucuba (spotted laurel)	Evergreen shrub	*In the first spring after planting, cut back the previous year's growth by around one third to encourage bushiness. Once established, remove overlong, wayward and straggly shoots and winter die-back in midspring.*
Berberis (barberry)	Evergreen/deciduous shrub	*Regular pruning is not necessary. Evergreen types can be pruned after flowering, if the berries are not wanted; otherwise prune in late autumn or winter after the berries have gone. Deciduous forms are best thinned out each year after flowering, to a low framework of permanent branches; remove some shoots down to their base.*
Betula (birch)	Deciduous tree	*Prune from autumn to winter when fully dormant, otherwise these trees bleed sap very heavily.* *Upright, spreading trees can be trained as central-leader standards or as feathered trees (see p60). Once established, they need little pruning apart from the removal of unwanted growth. B. pendula can be grown as a central-leader standard, a feathered tree or a multistemmed tree (see p61). Hard pruning of most birches is not recommended.*
Brachyglottis (Dunedin Group) 'Sunshine' (syn. *Senecio* 'Sunshine')	Evergreen shrub	*Prune in spring as new growth starts to break and the worst of the winter frosts are over. Check for winter damage and remove any affected growth, as well as any wayward and thin branches. Hard pruning in spring to encourage a compact, bushy shape will result in a better foliage effect, but at the expense of flowers. Plants can also be pruned to shape after flowering.*

Plant name	Plant type	Pruning method
Buddleja alternifolia	Deciduous shrub	*This species flowers on the previous year's stems. Prune it after flowering, cutting back the flowered stems to healthy buds or non-flowered sideshoots.*
B. davidii (butterfly bush)	Deciduous shrub	*See full pruning details on p43.*
B. globosa (orange ball tree)	Semievergreen/ deciduous shrub	*This species flowers on the previous year's stems. It does not need regular pruning, but any should be done in late winter. Shorten wayward and very tall branches by one third.*
Buxus (box)	Evergreen shrub	*Responds well to clipping and readily shoots from old wood. Cut back young plants quite hard to encourage bushy growth. Trim mature plants from early to late summer, giving two cuts per year.*
Callicarpa (beauty berry)	Deciduous shrub	*Does not need regular pruning, but thin out older stems to their base to prevent the plant becoming congested. Remove one in three of the older stems in spring after there is little risk of frost but before growth starts.*
Callistemon (bottlebrush)	Evergreen shrub	*After planting, tip prune new plants to encourage bushy growth. Mature plants are best left unpruned but, in time, can become straggly, so cut back older stems to young shoots after flowering.*
Calluna (ling)	Evergreen shrub	*Prune annually after flowering to keep plants compact and to ensure long life and long flowering (see p49).*
Camellia	Evergreen shrub	*Flowers are produced on the previous year's growth. Prune young plants in spring to produce bushy growth by cutting back thin or leggy shoots to 2–3 buds or by removing the shoots completely. Established plants do not require regular pruning, but can be kept bushy by pruning immediately after flowering.*
Campsis (trumpet vine)	Deciduous climber	*Flowers are produced on the current year's growth. Establish a framework of branches in spring by pruning back all stems to 15cm (6in) above ground level to promote strong growth. Select two or three of the strongest shoots and tie them into the framework; remove the rest. Once established, prune annually in early to midspring before new growth starts. Cut back the previous year's growth to 2–3 buds from the established framework. Remove any weak or misplaced stems completely.*
Caragana	Deciduous shrub	*Flowers are produced on short shoots on two-year-old wood. Prune young plants in spring to encourage bushy growth. No further pruning is needed.*
Carpenteria	Evergreen shrub	*Prune after flowering to maintain bushiness and completely remove one in three of the older stems that have been weakened by flowering. More drastic pruning is often possible, but not recommended as plants take a long time to recover.*

Plant name	Plant type	Pruning method
Carpinus (hornbeam)	Deciduous tree	*Prune from late summer until midwinter; pruning at other times can lead to severe bleeding. Hornbeam can be grown as a central-leader standard, as a feathered tree (see p60) or pleached (see p72). Established trees need little pruning.*
Caryopteris (blue spiraea)	Deciduous shrub	*Flowers on the current year's growth. In the first spring after planting, prune hard to produce a low framework, preferably on a short leg. Thereafter, prune in mid- to late spring, as the growth buds are breaking, back to the resulting framework of branches, shortening all stems to within 2.5–5cm (1–2in) of the older wood. Do not cut into the older wood as plants rarely reshoot.*
Castanea (chestnut, sweet chestnut)	Deciduous tree	*Pruning should be carried out when dormant, although minor pruning can be done in late summer. Established trees need little in the way of pruning other than reducing the spread of mature branches by shortening them to prevent wind damage.*
Catalpa (bean tree)	Deciduous tree	*Pruning should be carried out when dormant, from autumn to late winter; frost-damaged growth can be removed from mid- to late spring. Train as a central-leader standard or as a branch-headed standard (see p60). Established trees need little pruning, but old, long, heavy branches may need to be shortened or removed to balance the framework.* *Bean tree responds well to hard pruning and C. bignonioides 'Aurea' is best treated this way to increase the size and quality of its foliage. It can also be pollarded, by cutting back branches every year or every other year in late winter (see p71).*
Ceanothus (California lilac)	Evergreen/deciduous shrub/wall shrub	*Time of pruning depends on flowering time: prune those that bloom in spring and early summer after flowering in midsummer; prune those that flower in summer and autumn in spring. Cut back the previous season's growth by one third to half. For wall training California lilac, see full pruning details on p96.*
Ceratostigma (hardy plumbago)	Deciduous/evergreen shrub	*Pruning should be carried out in midspring. If plants die back in winter, remove all dead wood and shorten remaining stems to 2.5–5cm (1–2in) above ground level.*
Cercidiphyllum japonicum (katsura tree)	Deciduous tree	*Grow with a single central leader or multistemmed (See p60); each tree will grow in its own preferred way, do not try to change it or prune into a different form. Multistemmed trees branch at an early age and need no formative pruning, although excessive and weak stems can be removed in autumn or winter when dormant. Central-leader trees may need the lower branches removed when dormant, to form a clear stem. Established trees need little or no pruning.*
Cercis (Judas tree, redbud)	Deciduous shrub/tree	*Prune in early summer. Grow as a multistemmed tree (see p61) or shrub with a framework of 3–5 well-spaced stems. Established trees need no pruning. C. canadensis can also be grown as a feathered tree (see p60) or on a 90cm (3ft) stem.*

167

Plant name	Plant type	Pruning method
Chaenomeles (flowering or Japanese quince, japonica)	Deciduous shrub	*See full pruning details on p97.*
Chimonanthus (wintersweet)	Deciduous/ semievergreen shrub	*Is best left unpruned – especially when young so that it can build up mature flowering growth. Even when established, little or no pruning is needed. If necessary, shoots can be thinned and older growth shortened by up to 30cm (12in) after flowering, but keep this to a minimum or the following winter's display will be reduced.*
Choisya (Mexican orange blossom)	Evergreen shrub	*Little or no regular pruning is needed, although cutting back those shoots that have flowered in spring can encourage further flowering. Frosted shoots can be removed at the same time.*
Cistus (sun rose, rock rose)	Evergreen shrub	*After planting, prune plants to encourage bushiness; tall shoots are best shortened by up to two thirds back to sideshoots. Established plants need little or no pruning, but dead and damaged shoots can be removed after flowering, together with any wayward growth.*
Clematis	Deciduous/ evergreen climber	*See full pruning details on p88.*
Clerodendrum	Evergreen/deciduous shrub	*C. trichotomum is best grown with a single stem. It can be pruned in spring before the buds break. This will reduce the amount of flowers and fruit, but increase the size of leaves. C. bungei may die back in winter and so should be hard pruned in spring at bud break. Where growth is retained through winter, cut back to a framework of branches 60–90cm (2–3ft) above ground level.*
Colutea (bladder senna)	Deciduous shrub	*Needs little or no annual pruning, other than removing unwanted growth in spring. Bladder senna responds well to hard pruning and, if necessary, you can cut back the branches to within a few buds of their base.*
Convolvulus cneorum	Evergreen shrub	*Plants do not need regular pruning, but overlong and wayward shoots can be cut back to their base or a healthy sideshoot in early spring before the buds break. Shoots affected by winter die-back can be cut out at the same time. C. cneorum does not respond well to hard pruning.*
Cornus (dogwood, Cornelian cherry)	Deciduous shrub	*For shrubby dogwoods see full pruning details on p44. Pruning of the Cornelian cherry (C. mas) is carried out in early summer, but keep this to a minimum by just thinning out unwanted stems.*

Plant name	Plant type	Pruning method
Cornus alternifolia, *C. controversa,* *C. florida,* *C. kousa*	Deciduous tree	C. alternifolia *and* C. controversa *are trained as a central-leader standard (see p60). From autumn to early spring, remove competing leaders and low sideshoots in the first two or three years; plants need little in the way of pruning afterwards.* C. alternifolia *can also be grown as a multistemmed, feathered tree (see p60).* C. florida *and* C. kousa *are best grown on a short leg, up to 90cm (3ft) long, by removing all sideshoots to this height from autumn to early spring. Thereafter they are best left unpruned.*
Coronilla	Evergreen/deciduous shrub	*Little pruning is needed, apart from removing old and unwanted growth at the base of the plant after flowering. Plants do not respond well to hard pruning.*
Corylopsis (winter hazel)	Deciduous shrub	*Does not need regular pruning, apart from removing dead growth; in fact, pruning can spoil its otherwise attractive shape. Long and wayward branches can be cut back to their base, if absolutely necessary, after flowering.*
Corylus (hazel)	Deciduous shrub	*Shrubby hazels are grown as multistemmed bushes. To ensure there is a good balance of new and mature growth, remove one or two of the oldest stems at ground level in late winter. Plants can also be coppiced (see p70).*
Cotinus (smoke bush)	Deciduous shrub	*Prune in late winter or early spring before growth starts. In the first spring after planting, cut back growth made the previous year by about one third to help create a well-branched shrub. The flowers are produced on two- to three-year-old wood, and usually only in hot summers. To encourage flowers, keep pruning to a minimum, just thin out overcrowded shoots. To encourage foliage displays, cut back the stems by half to three quarters; the harder you prune the better the foliage. For the best of both worlds, cut out one stem in three in spring, starting with the oldest.*

169

Cercis canadensis can be grown successfully as a multistemmed tree or shrub with a framework of 3–5 well-spaced stems.

Dogwoods (Cornus) cultivated for their colourful stems require hard pruning each year to promote the strongest colours.

How and when you prune clematis depends on when it flowers. Find out the full details on p88.

Plant name	Plant type	Pruning method
Cotoneaster	Evergreen/deciduous shrub	*Needs only minimal pruning, to keep it within bounds: thin out unwanted growth and remove any damaged shoots. Deciduous forms can be pruned from winter to midspring, evergreens in spring.*
Crataegus (hawthorn, thorn tree)	Deciduous tree	*Prune any time from autumn to early spring. Common hawthorn (C. monogyna), Midland hawthorn (C. laevigata), their varieties and less common C. tanacetifolia can be grown as a central-leader or branch-headed standard (see p60) or a multistemmed tree (see p61). Established trees need little in the way of further pruning, apart from thinning out overcrowded and rubbing branches.*
Cytisus (broom)	Deciduous shrub	*Flowers on growth produced the previous year. After planting, lightly cut back or pinch out the growing tips to encourage a bushy habit. Prune annually after flowering, removing the faded flowers and reducing the flowering stems by two thirds of the previous year's growth. Avoid cutting back hard, because new shoots will not be produced when plants are cut back into old wood.*
C. battandieri (pineapple broom)	Semievergreen wall shrub	*Flowers are produced on the current year's growth. Little or no pruning is needed other than removing dead or damaged stems. Wayward stems can be cut back to the main framework. Pruning should be carried out after flowering.*
Daboecia (heath)	Evergreen shrub	*Clip back plants after flowering to remove all the spent flowers and a small amount of leafy growth below them.*
Danae (Alexandrian laurel)	Evergreen shrub	*In late spring, prune unwanted stems to ground level. To restrict plants that have suckered and spread too far, remove the suckers (see p69).*
Daphne	Evergreen/deciduous shrub	*Needs minimal pruning and is best left unpruned as it can suffer from die-back; completely remove any die-back as soon as seen. Prune only to remove damaged, diseased or wayward growth; this should be carried out in early spring or immediately after flowering. D. odora and D. cneorum tolerate light trimming to maintain a compact habit.*
Davidia (handkerchief tree)	Deciduous tree	*The bracts are produced on the previous year's growth. Trees naturally form a strong, central leader, with strong, upright sideshoots. These may overtake the leader, so should be removed from autumn to early spring until there is a clear stem of the desired height. Established trees usually need no regular attention, and they do not respond to hard pruning and are reluctant to reshoot.*
Desfontainea spinosa	Evergreen shrub	*Pruning should be kept to a minimum – just removing dead, damaged and a few unwanted branches in spring.*

170

Plant name	Plant type	Pruning method
Deutzia	Deciduous shrub	*Flowers are produced on new shoots from the previous year's growth. After planting, tip back the young shoots, to encourage bushy growth (see p38). All further pruning is carried out after flowering. Prune to young shoots below the growth that has flowered. As plants get older, remove some of the oldest branches to ground level or to a strong, low-growing shoot.*
Elaeagnus (oleaster)	Evergreen/deciduous shrub	*Does not need regular/annual pruning as it naturally produces well-shaped plants. Wayward branches or unwanted growth should be removed in summer – after flowering for the deciduous species and in late summer for the evergreens. Tolerates hard pruning and can be pruned back into old wood if needed.*
Enkianthus (pagoda bush)	Deciduous shrub	*No regular pruning is needed. Plants can be deadheaded after flowering, and crowded branches can be thinned out at the same time. Leggy and overgrown plants respond well to hard pruning after flowering.*
Erica (heather)	Evergreen shrub	*See full puning details on p49.* *Cut back tree heath (E. arborea) by up to two thirds in the first two or three years, to promote bushy growth. Afterwards, plants need little pruning, but overlong shoots can be cut back, if needed, after flowering.*
Escallonia	Evergreen shrub	*Flowers on the previous year's growth. During the first few years, prune lightly to encourage bushy growth. After that, no regular pruning is needed, but cut back any shoots that spoil the symmetry. Pruning is carried out after flowering, although if flowering finishes late in the year it is better to leave pruning until the following spring.*
Eucalyptus (gum)	Evergreen tree	*Pruning should be carried out in spring after there is little risk of hard frosts. Train trees as central-leader standards (see p60), although the leader may lose its dominance as the tree matures, to produce a multibranched effect. Some species naturally form multistemmed trees. All can be hard pruned, even cut back to a stump just above ground level if they are damaged. Some, such as E. gunnii and E. pauciflora subsp. niphophila, are grown as pollarded or coppiced shrubs (see p70).*
Eucryphia	Evergreen tree	*Does not need or like much pruning and does not respond to hard pruning.*
Euonymus	Evergreen/deciduous shrub	*Prune deciduous forms in late winter or early spring, cutting out the older stems to ground level, to help open up the centre. Cut back evergreens from mid- to late spring, to remove unwanted growth.*
Exochorda	Deciduous shrub	*Flowers on the previous year's growth. Established plants can be pruned annually after flowering to remove weak growth and reduce overcrowding. Cut out one in three of the oldest stems to ground level.*

Plant name	Plant type	Pruning method
Fagus (beech)	Deciduous tree	*Pruning should be carried out from autumn to early spring. Plants should be trained as feathered trees (see p60) to promote a strong leader. After a few years, the sideshoots produced low down on the main stem can be cleared to form the main trunk; this should be done over several years and not all in one go. As the crown develops, remove any competing leaders. Established trees rarely need any further formative pruning.*
Fallopia baldschuanica (syn. *Polygonum baldschuanicum*) (Russian vine, mile-a-minute)	Deciduous climber	*Needs no formative pruning, simply space out the stems on the support to provide even coverage. Established plants tend to form an entangled mass of stems, making careful pruning difficult. Cut back all stems by around one third of their length in late winter or early spring.*
× *Fatshedera lizei*	Evergreen shrub	*Little or no pruning is needed apart from removing dead, damaged or unwanted growth in spring.*
Fatsia japonica (false castor oil plant)	Evergreen shrub	*Needs little in the way of pruning, although winter-damaged shoots should be removed in late spring. Sparse and unwanted branches are best removed completely to ground level in spring.*
Forsythia	Deciduous shrub	*Pruning should be carried out after flowering. Keep pruning to a minimum during the first two or three years after planting. However, once established, prune annually after flowering, by thinning out overcrowded stems at the centre of the plant and cutting out one in three of the main stems at the base, starting with the oldest. Older plants that are not pruned become woody at the base and produce fewer flowers.*
Fothergilla	Deciduous shrub	*Little or no annual pruning is needed other than the removal of dead or diseased stems and the thinning out of any congested growth as the flowers fade.*
Fraxinus (ash)	Deciduous tree	*Usually requires little formative pruning as it naturally produces a central leader and subsequent crown (see p60). Mature trees need little pruning apart from removing damaged branches and water shoots that form around damaged growth (see p68); do this when the tree is dormant between autumn and early spring.* *F. angustifolia 'Raywood' can be grown as a central-leader standard or as a feathered tree (see p60).* *Weeping ash (F. excelsior 'Pendula') is grown as a weeping standard (see p60), and should be pruned only lightly to remove crossing branches and an even spacing of branches.*
Fremontodendron	Evergreen wall shrub	*Flowers on the current year's growth. Once the main framework has been established, little or no pruning is usually needed other than the removal of dead or damaged stems after flowering; also shorten wayward stems and outward-growing shoots, cutting back to sideshoots that grow parallel to the wall.*

172

Plant name	Plant type	Pruning method
Fuchsia	Deciduous shrub	*Pinch out the tips of young plants to encourage bushy growth. In spring, if the top growth has been killed, cut plants back to near ground level. In mild areas, top growth may survive, in which case remove any dead growth and thin out congested stems.*
Garrya elliptica (silk-tassel bush)	Evergreen wall shrub	*After planting, prune to retain two or three main framework stems, and cut back all sideshoots that are growing away from the support. Once established and the framework or support is covered, cut back any badly place shoots in early or midspring as the catkins fade, but before new growth begins.*
Gaultheria (syn. *Pernettya*)	Evergreen shrub	*Little pruning is needed, although plants can be trimmed back after flowering in spring and suckers can be removed to restrict their spread (see p69).*
Genista (broom)	Deciduous shrub	*Produces its colourful, pea-like flowers in spring or summer on growth that is two years old. Cut back after flowering to keep the plants bushy and compact, removing the growth that has flowered.* *Most brooms do not produce new growth if they are cut back hard into old, brown wood.*
Gleditsia (honey locust)	Deciduous tree	*Trees rarely need formative training and pruning and even mature trees can be left unpruned, apart from removing dead or damaged wood in spring. Pruning should be carried out from late summer to early winter.*
Griselinia	Evergreen shrub	*Little or no regular pruning is needed, but being susceptible to frost it may need to have any dead or damaged growth removed in spring.*
× *Halimiocistus* and *Halimium*	Evergreen shrub	*After planting, prune plants to encourage bushiness; cut tall shoots by up to two thirds back to sideshoots. Established plants need little or no pruning, but dead and damaged shoots can be removed after flowering, together with any wayward growth.*
Hamamelis (witch hazel)	Deciduous shrub	*Keep pruning to a minimum, apart from the removal of dead or diseased branches after flowering, and other stems to maintain the shape. Always cut back to a healthy sideshoot lower down the stem.*
Hebe	Evergreen shrub	*Prune hebe grown for its foliage rather than its flowers in spring, to achieve a compact and neat habit. Plants grown for flowers and foliage should be pruned only in mid- or late spring as new growth starts. Plants can be hard pruned if they become too topheavy, depending on their age and health.*
Hedera (ivy)	Evergreen climber	*Prune during early spring before new growth starts to keep plants within bounds and to ensure they are tidy. Cut back wayward shoots to just above a bud. Remove overcrowded shoots entirely as well as those growing away from the support.*

Plant name	Plant type	Pruning method
Helianthemum (rock rose)	Evergreen shrub	*Pinch back young plants after planting, to encourage bushy growth. Lightly prune established plants after flowering to remove flowering stems and prevent the build-up of unproductive stems.*
Helichrysum italicum (curry plant)	Evergreen shrub	*In spring, remove winter-damaged stems and cut back leggy shoots to just above old wood.*
Hibiscus	Deciduous shrub	*Flowers on the current year's growth. Young plants should be cut back by half to two thirds after planting to encourage bushy growth. Pruning established plants is best kept to a minimum, but unwanted growth can be removed in late spring.*
Hippophae rhamnoides (sea buckthorn)	Deciduous shrub	*Little pruning is needed, apart from thinning out unwanted stems to ground level in summer, if plants become too thick, and removing unwanted suckers from the periphery of the plant (see p69).*
Humulus (hop)	Deciduous climber	*In early or mid-spring, cut back all of last year's shoots to ground level and tie in new shoots around the base of the support.*
Hydrangea anomala subsp. *petiolaris* (climbing hydrangea)	Deciduous wall shrub	*Tie in young shoots to their supports until they become self-supporting. Little or no routine pruning is required, and pruning is best kept to a minimum, apart from removing the flowered shoots after flowering. At the same time, reduce overlong shoots and outward-growing sideshoots by cutting to a healthy bud.*
H. arborescens, *H. paniculata*	Deciduous shrub	*These flower better if pruned annually in spring to a low framework 30–60cm (1–2ft) high. In the first spring after planting, cut back all new growth to within 5cm (2in) of the old wood. Then each year, cut back all the previous year's growth to the lowest pair of buds where it joins the main framework of branches. If this is too severe, reduce the stem by about half.*
H. aspera, *H. quercifolia*, *H. sargentiana*, *H. villosa*	Deciduous shrub	*Produce their flowers on the current year's growth. Need minimal pruning; any work should be carried out in spring.*
H. macrophylla (mophead and lacecap hydrangeas)	Deciduous shrub	*Lacecaps and mopheads produce their flowers on the previous year's growth. For mopheads see full pruning details on p41. Lacecaps need less pruning, although faded flowerheads can be cut back to the second pair of leaves below the head, in spring.*
Hypericum (St John's wort)	Evergreen/deciduous shrub	*Flowers on the current year's growth. Pruning is carried out in spring. For the shrubby hypericums, remove old, damaged and thin shoots and reduce remaining stems to 5–10cm (2–4in) above ground level or to strong sideshoots. H. androsaemum and H. × inodorum are best pruned only every 2–3 years rather than annually. Rose of Sharon (H. calycinum) can have all the previous year's growth cut back with shears to within a few centimetres (inches) of ground level.*

Plant name	Plant type	Pruning method
Ilex (holly)	Evergreen shrub/tree	*Hollies grown as shrubs need little pruning, apart from shaping, but any that is needed should be carried out in late summer. When grown as trees, young plants should be trained as central-leader standards or feathered trees (see p60). If required, keep the pyramidal shape by removing unwanted shoots. Established trees do not need regular or maintenance pruning, but any that is required can be carried out from mid- to late summer.*
Indigofera (indigo)	Deciduous shrub	*Flowers on the current year's growth. In warm areas, little or no annual pruning is needed. In colder regions, remove weak, frosted, damaged or diseased stems and thin out congested growth near to ground level in midspring.*
Jasminum humile, J. parkeri (shrubby jasmine)	Evergreen/deciduous shrub	*These flower at the end of shoots produced the previous year. Do not prune in the first few years after planting. Once established, remove one or two of the old stems after flowering. Every few years, prune out one in three stems, starting with the oldest.*
J. nudiflorum (winter jasmine)	Deciduous wall shrub	*Flowers on the previous year's shoots. Start by creating a framework of well-spaced branches; it may pay to cut back the plant by up to two thirds after flowering, to produce strong basal growth. Once established, prune immediately after flowering each year. Shorten to 2–3 buds any shoots that are not needed to extend the framework.*
J. officinale (common jasmine, summer jasmine)	Deciduous climber	*Flowers on sideshoots from the previous year's growth and terminally on new growth. Create a framework of well-spaced branches over the support; if needed, cut back the plant by up to two thirds after flowering, to produce strong basal growth. Once established, cut out overcrowded growth and weak shoots and prune flowered shoots to a sideshoot or bud near their base after flowering. Other jasmines treated in the same way include J. beesianum, J. polyanthum and J. × stephanense.*

Cut back young hibiscus plants by half to two thirds after planting, to encourage bushy growth.

Hollies (Ilex) grown as shrubs need little regular or maintenance pruning, apart from shaping carried out during late summer.

Keep pruning to a minimum as mophead hydrangeas do not like or need regular pruning. Find out full details on p41.

PRUNING DIRECTORY

Plant name	Plant type	Pruning method
Juglans (walnut)	Deciduous tree	*Remove sideshoots from the trunk when the tree is young, to reduce blemishes and cavities. Pruning is best kept to a minimum on established trees and any pruning must be carried out from midsummer to early autumn; pruning in late winter or spring can cause severe bleeding.*
Kalmia (calico bush)	Evergreen shrub	*Needs very little pruning, but deadheading is usually worthwhile after flowering if it is achievable.*
Kerria	Deciduous shrub	*See full pruning details on p39.*
Koelreuteria	Deciduous tree	*Keep pruning to a minimum. Do not tip prune to encourage bushy growth and do not hard prune. Any pruning, simply to remove dead, damaged and dying growth, is best carried out during winter.*
Kolkwitzia (beauty bush)	Deciduous shrub	*Flowers on two-year-old wood. Allow young plants to develop with little or no thinning. Established plants sucker freely and can be pruned after flowering to remove one in three of the oldest stems. Either cut these out at ground level or to a low sideshoot.*
Laburnum (golden chain, golden rain)	Deciduous tree	*Pruning is best carried out from late summer to late autumn. Golden rain can be grown as a feathered tree or a central-leader standard (see p60). Prune shoots when they are young, as removing large branches can lead to cavities and other problems. Do not prune established trees apart from spur pruning (see p130) to promote flowering – cutting back sideshoots to 2–3 leaves or buds.* *The weeping L. alpinum 'Pendulum' and L. anagyroides are grown as top-grafted weeping standards (see p60).*
Laurus (bay, sweet bay, bay laurel)	Evergreen tree	*Grows naturally as a central-leader tree (see p60) or can be trained as a feathered tree (see p60) or treated as a shrub and trained as a rounded bush, pyramid or lollipop standard (see p55). Pruning should be carried out in spring, just as new growth begins; light trimming and shaping can also be done in summer.*
Lavandula (lavender)	Evergreen shrub	*See full pruning details on p48.*
Lavatera (tree mallow)	Deciduous shrub	*Flowers on the current year's growth. Older wood is not very strong, so cut back plants in early autumn by one third to prevent windrock. In spring, once there is little risk of severe frosts and the buds are beginning to break, cut stems back hard to 15–30cm (6–12in) above ground level, to form a stubby framework, or to within a few buds of the previous year's growth. Any damaged and weak growth can also be removed during the growing season.*
Leptospermum (tea tree)	Evergreen shrub	*After planting, tip prune shoots to ensure a bushy habit. In subsequent years, trim shoots lightly in spring to prevent leggy growth. Plants do not shoot from old growth, so avoid cutting into old wood; neglected plants are best replaced.*

Plant name	Plant type	Pruning method
Lespedeza (bush clover)	Deciduous shrub	*Produces its pea-like flowers in late summer and autumn on the current year's growth. Little pruning is needed, but plants are usually killed down to ground level in winter by severe weather. Once there is little risk of frost, cut down all dead stems to ground level or back to healthy growth.*
Leucothoe	Evergreen shrub	*Needs minimal pruning, although one or two of the oldest stems can be cut down to their base in late spring if needed.*
Leycesteria (Himalayan honeysuckle, pheasant berry)	Deciduous shrub	*Produces thick clumps of stems, which should be thinned out in spring, cutting weak, old and damaged stems to ground level. If left unpruned, plants soon become congested.*
Ligustrum (privet)	Evergreen/deciduous shrub	*Although privet is usually thought of as a hedging plant, there are several species that are ornamental enough to be grown as specimens: for example, L. japonicum, L. lucidum and variegated varieties of common privet (L. ovalifolium). No pruning is needed after planting. Keep subsequent pruning to a minimum, tidying up plants and removing unwanted growth in spring.*
Liquidambar (sweet gum)	Deciduous tree	*When grown as a central-leader standard (see p60), remove competing leaders as soon as seen. Little or no pruning is needed apart from removing unwanted branches from late autumn to early spring; dead wood can also be cut out in late summer.*
Liriodendron (tulip tree)	Deciduous tree	*Little if any formative pruning is needed, and pruning of established trees should be kept to a minimum. If pruning is needed, do it from autumn to early spring, although dead wood can be removed when the tree is in full leaf.*
Lonicera (honeysuckle)	Deciduous/ evergreen/semi-evergreen climber	*See full pruning details on p94.*
L. fragrantissima, L. korolkowii, L. nitida, L. pileata, L. × purpusii L. tatarica (shrubby honeysuckle)	Evergreen/deciduous shrub	*Pruning depends on the reason the plant is grown and, if a flowering species, the time of flowering.* *L. nitida is an evergreen grown for its foliage, especially golden-leaved L.n. 'Baggesen's Gold'; it produces small, creamy-white flowers. Plants can be trimmed up to three times a year between mid- to late spring and autumn, to keep them compact and bushy. L. pileata is similar but needs minimal pruning.* *L. tatarica and L. korolkowii bear summer flowers on the previous year's growth, often followed by colourful berries. L. fragrantissima and L. × purpusii are winter-flowering species. Both types should be pruned after flowering, removing old and weak stems at their base, and shortening up to one in three of the remaining shoots, to help keep them compact and bushy.* *All types can be renovated by pruning back to a low framework of branches or to within 15cm (6in) of the ground in early spring.*

177

Plant name	Plant type	Pruning method
Magnolia	Deciduous shrub	*Established magnolias usually do not need regular pruning – and they do not generally respond well to pruning. However, where damaged branches or overgrown plants need pruning, this should be carried out when the tree is in full leaf, usually during midsummer. In spring and early summer the wounds will bleed, and pruning in the dormant season often leads to die-back. Heavy flowering and seed production can reduce the plant's vigour – especially small plants – so try and deadhead if possible.*
M. campbellii, M. delavayi, M. denudata, M. kobus	Deciduous/ evergreen tree	*Although most magnolias are classed as shrubs, a few species are tree-like in their growth. The general principles of pruning are the same; see p40 for details.* *M. campbellii and M. kobus produce pyramidal trees with a strong central leader. Any pruning should be carried out in summer. Only prune out competing leaders and damaged growth; hard pruning produces vertical shoots that spoil the overall shape. As the plant matures, lower branches can be removed over a number of years if required, otherwise no further pruning is usually needed. M. kobus may produce water shoots (see p68), which should be removed as soon as they are noticed.* *Old, neglected plants may be successfully renovated by pruning back all the branches to the main framework, but this should be done over a three-year period.* *M. delavayi and M. denudata when grown as trees are similar, but often produce long, thin branches, which can spoil the shape. These should be pruned back in spring as growth begins.*
M. grandiflora	Evergreen tree/wall shrub	*This handsome, evergreen tree produces creamy white flowers in late summer. In cool climates, it is often trained against a sunny, sheltered wall. After planting, tie the leading shoot vertically to support wires, secure the sideshoots at an angle of 45 degrees and cut out all forward- and backward-facing shoots. In the second year, lower the sideshoots and tie them in horizontally. Any new sideshoots can also be trained at 45 degrees. In subsequent years, continue to attach the sideshoots to the support wires – initially at an angle and then the following year horizontally. Tie in shoots to fill in the framework and in summer remove unwanted shoots. Once the allotted space has been filled, prune out the shoot tips in summer.*
Mahonia	Evergreen shrub	*Flowers on growth produced the previous year, so prune after flowering. New plants can be encouraged to develop a branching, attractive habit by cutting out the growing tips after flowering; remove the top rosette of leaves along with the spent flowerheads. No regular pruning is needed, but established plants can be kept within bounds and flowering well by pruning out one in three stems, starting with the oldest. Low-growing M. aquifolium, when used as ground cover, can be cut back hard each year during late spring.*

178

Plant name	Plant type	Pruning method
Malus (crab apple)	Deciduous tree	Pruning can be carried out any time from autumn to early spring. When grown as a standard, little formative pruning is needed once the framework branches are formed. Future pruning usually consists only of removing badly placed, crossing or unwanted branches. Crab apples do not respond well to hard pruning.
Morus alba (white mulberry)	Deciduous tree	Maintain the central leader for as long as possible, or train in a replacement if it fails. As the tree matures, the uppermost sideshoots will naturally overtake the leader to form a broad-headed tree. Pruning is best kept to a minimum.
Nandina domestica (heavenly bamboo, sacred bamboo)	Evergreen shrub	On planting, cut back spindly plants to promote bushy growth. Established plants need little pruning, apart from keeping the plant tidy in spring.
Nothofagus (southern beech)	Deciduous/evergreen tree	Evergreen species tend to produce dual leaders, so remove the weakest at the earliest opportunity. Established trees need no regular pruning. Evergreen pruning is carried out in late spring. With deciduous species it is important to maintain a single, strong leader; lower branches may also need to be removed. Prune from autumn to early spring.
Nyssa (tupelo, sour gum)	Deciduous tree	In cool climates, trees often lose their leader and grow as multistemmed trees with a framework of branches on a short stem (see p61). In warmer climates, they can be grown as central-leader trees (see p60). All pruning should be carried out when the tree is dormant, from late autumn to early spring.
Olearia (daisy bush)	Evergreen shrub	After planting, shorten long shoots to encourage a bushy habit. Once established, keep pruning to a minimum, apart from removing damaged, especially winter-damaged, growth. To keep plants within bounds, prune stems on the summer-flowering species by one third to one half in spring, once new growth begins; do this after flowering on spring-flowering species.
Osmanthus	Evergreen shrub	Once established, prune to remove winter-damaged growth and to keep plants within bounds by cutting back overlong shoots. All types are pruned in spring – the summer-flowering ones once new growth begins, and those that flower in spring after flowering.
Ozothamnus	Evergreen shrub	Needs little pruning, apart from removing damaged growth in spring. Ozothamnus tolerates hard pruning, so neglected plants can be cut back hard.
Pachysandra	Evergreen shrub	Needs little pruning, apart from removing unwanted growth after flowering. Should a plant become bare and woody, shorten its stems to 5–7.5cm (2–3in) above ground level in late spring.

179

Plant name	Plant type	Pruning method
Paeonia (tree peony)	Deciduous shrub	*Needs little pruning, but you should cut off the faded flowers when they have finished or, if you want seeds, after the seeds have been gathered in autumn. It is also worth removing some of the very old, leggy stems of mature plants by pruning them back to ground level in summer.*
Parrotia persica (Persian ironwood)	Deciduous tree	*Plants either develop a central leader and can be grown as a tree (see p60) or, in some cases, this leader is lost and the plant develops a shrubby habit. Both types develop naturally with little or no formative pruning and should be allowed to grow in whichever way they take. Unwanted and damaged growth can be removed any time from autumn to early spring.*
Parthenocissus (Boston ivy, Virginia creeper)	Deciduous climber	*Plants need no formative pruning, but new shoots should be tied to support wires for the first couple of years. Once established, give plants an annual tidy up in autumn, after the foliage has fallen, or in early winter to keep them within bounds. Virginia creeper can also be lightly trimmed in summer.*
Passiflora (passion flower)	Evergreen/ semievergreen climber	*Establish a framework of stems 15–20cm (6–8in) apart on a sturdy support. To fan train (see p129), nip out the growing points after planting to encourage shoots from the base and tie in up to five of the strongest shoots to form the fan shape. If training along support wires, select a main stem to grow vertically and pinch back sideshoots until the main stem has reached the top of the support. Then train sideshoots horizontally to form the framework.* *Prune established plants in spring, removing dead, damaged and overcrowded stems and shortening any others to keep each plant within bounds. Then cut back new growth to within 15cm (6in) of the established framework. After flowering, cut back the flowered shoots to within 2–3 leaves of the framework branches.*
Paulownia (foxglove tree)	Deciduous tree	*If growing as a central-leader standard (see p60), rub out the buds that appear on the lower 1.2–1.5m (4–5ft) of stem, rather than pruning out the subsequent branches. Further pruning should be to remove damaged and unwanted growth. Do all pruning from midspring to early summer.* *It is often better to grow foxglove tree as a coppiced or pollarded shrub (see pp70–72) for its foliage. Prune to encourage this.*
Penstemon	Evergreen shrub	*The dwarf and prostrate species need minimal pruning, but can be sheared over. The taller, border types should be pruned annually, especially to enhance the upright growth habit. Prune in spring once there is little risk of severe frosts.*
Perovskia (Russian sage)	Deciduous shrub	*Flowers at the ends of the current year's growth. Plants should be pruned annually in spring as new growth is appearing. Cut back all the previous year's growth to 5–10cm (2–4in) above ground level in the first few years, and then to a framework of old wood that develops in subsequent years.*

180

Plant name	Plant type	Pruning method
Philadelphus (mock orange, orange blossom)	Deciduous shrub	*Prune immediately after flowering in summer. Plants produce new growth from the ground that can, in time, become very crowded. Therefore, once established, prune out one in four of the oldest stems annually, by removing them at ground level or to a low-growing sideshoot.* P. microphyllus *is a smaller shrub that needs little pruning, but excessive and congested growth can be removed after flowering.*
Phlomis	Evergreen shrub	*After planting, remove any weak growth and shorten overlong and straggly stems. After that, established plants do not need regular pruning, apart from removing winter-damaged and long, leggy or wayward stems, by cutting back to a healthy bud or shoot. Old and weak stems should be completely removed. All pruning is done in spring when the plant is actively growing.* *Neglected plants can be renovated by cutting back hard to within 7.5–15cm (3–6in) of the ground or, for older plants, a higher framework of branches.*
Photinia	Evergreen/deciduous shrub	*Does not need regular pruning, although the evergreen species are often used for hedging, which will need annual tidying and shaping. The evergreens can have shoots cut back by up to 15cm (6in) in spring, to encourage the brightly coloured, young foliage. Deciduous species can have overcrowded growth removed in winter.*
Phygelius (Cape figwort)	Evergreen/ semievergreen shrub	*Produces flowers from summer to autumn on the current year's growth. After planting, cut back plants to encourage bushy growth. In cold regions, prune stems that have been damaged by cold weather and frost back to buds on live growth or, if needed, to the base of the plant. This should be done in spring once there is little risk of frosts. In milder climates, prune plants lightly in spring.*

If Osmanthus × burkwoodii *needs pruning, carry it out in late spring after flowering has finished.*

Virginia creeper (Parthenocissus) is a rampant climber that can be pruned when dormant to keep it within bounds.

To grow foxglove tree (Paulownia) for its flowers, keep pruning to a minimum, apart from removing damaged and unwanted growth.

Plant name	Plant type	Pruning method
Physocarpus opulifolius	Deciduous shrub	*Prune immediately after flowering in summer. Plants produce new growth from the ground and, in time, this can become very crowded and results in poor flowering. Therefore, once established, prune out one in four of the oldest stems annually, by removing them at ground level or to a low-growing shoot.*
Pieris	Evergreen shrub	*Deadhead after flowering. Frosted and winter-damaged growth can be removed at the same time, as can any uneven, overlong and lopsided growth. Other than this, plants need little pruning.*
Pittosporum	Evergreen shrub	*Needs little pruning, although removing winter-damaged growth, some thinning out and trimming can be done in midspring, when new growth has started.*
Platanus (plane)	Deciduous tree	*Can be hard pruned and is often pollarded annually (see p71). Pruning should be carried out from autumn to early spring. You can either clear the main trunk up to a height of 2.5–3m (8–10ft) or, to have branches down to ground level, remove sideshoots to 1.2m (4ft) and prune remaining sideshoots to downward-facing buds. Cut out strong, upright shoots so they do not compete with the leading shoot.*
Populus (poplar)	Deciduous tree	*Prune in late summer or early autumn, as poplars will bleed if pruned in late winter or early spring. Most are grown as central-leader standards with well-spaced sideshoots (see p60), although P. nigra 'Italica' is grown as a feathered tree (see p60) whose young sideshoots can be shortened to produce bushier growth. No regular pruning is needed.* *P. × jackii 'Aurora' (syn. P. × candicans 'Aurora') is grown as a central-leader or branch-headed standard (see p60) but, especially in a small garden, can be grown as a coppiced or pollarded, multistemmed shrub (see pp70–72).*
Potentilla	Deciduous shrub	*Flowers on the current year's growth. Prune annually in spring, as potentilla tends to become twiggy and unkempt if not pruned regularly. Cut back the oldest stems to their base, remove weak, twiggy growth and shorten young, vigorous shoots by up to one half. Plants can also be trimmed over after flowering.*
Prunus (cherry, cherry laurel)	Evergreen/deciduous shrub	*Deciduous species are grown for their spring flowers, produced on the previous year's growth, and sometimes for their excellent, autumn leaf tints. The evergreens are popular for their large, leathery leaves and fragrant, spring or summer flowers.* *Prune deciduous species in late spring and evergreens in late spring or early summer; autumn and winter pruning must be avoided to prevent problems from diseases.* *Pruning is best kept to a minimum – apart from P. glandulosa and those cherries used as hedging plants. These two species require regular pruning to ensure there are plenty of flowers. Evergreens usually need pruning to shape and to remove wayward growth, cutting back to a sideshoot.*

Plant name	Plant type	Pruning method
Prunus (ornamental cherry)	Deciduous tree	*Pruning is best kept to a minimum and always carried out in summer. If formative pruning is necessary, do it as soon as possible, making all pruning wounds as small as possible; large wounds are perfect sites for disease entry. Established trees usually need little in the way of pruning and prefer not to be pruned.* *The species cherries are usually grown as a central-leader standard with evenly, well-spaced sideshoots (see p60). On those cherries grown for their attractive bark, such as P. serrula, remove young shoots and branches forming on the main trunk or rub them out at an early age to show off the bark to its best advantage. The various varieties of Japanese flowering cherries differ in their growth habits and are either grown as central-leader, branch-headed or weeping standards (see p61) and need little if any pruning.*
Pyracantha (firethorn)	Evergreen shrub	*Requires little formative pruning or cutting back when established, apart from removing wayward and overlong shoots that spoil the shape, in spring.* *Although usually pruned in spring, wall-trained plants can be pruned for a second time from mid- to late summer, shortening the new growth to expose the developing berries and so make the most of the display.*
Pyrus (ornamental pear)	Deciduous tree	*Prune between autumn and early spring. P. calleryana, willow-leaved pear (P. salicifolia) and its widely available weeping variety P. s. 'Pendula' are grown with a clear stem of 1.5–1.6m (5–6ft), although the species can be left with shoots intact, to provide foliage to the ground. Formative prune by thinning out sideshoots in the head to create an evenly spaced and balanced framework of branches. Established trees do not need further pruning, but light trimming or the removal of young, unwanted branches can be carried out.*
Quercus (oak)	Deciduous/evergreen tree	*Train as a central-leader standard with even and well-spaced sideshoots. Established plants need little in the way of pruning, which, if needed, can be carried out between autumn and early spring.* *Evergreen Q. ilex looks shrubby when young and should be trained as a feathered tree (see p60). It does produce a central leader, and lower branches are shed naturally to produce a single-stemmed tree. Prune in summer, just removing damaged growth and trimming out winter damage.*
Rhododendron (azalea and rhododendron)	Evergreen/deciduous shrub	*Most rhododendrons need little pruning other than the removal of dead and unwanted growth, which should be shortened to a sideshoot or bud after flowering. Deciduous azaleas may benefit from having very old, unproductive shoots cut out.*

Plant name	Plant type	Pruning method

Rhus (sumach)	Deciduous shrub/tree	*Plants grown as shrubs can be left mainly unpruned, but thin out crowded shoots in early spring. R. typhina 'Dissecta' and other similar varieties are best hard pruned annually or every other year to enhance their cut or fern-like foliage. Shorten stems to 15cm (6in) above ground level or cut back to a low framework of woody stems.*
		   To grow as a standard tree (see p55), train a main stem upwards and remove other stems and sideshoots to produce a clear stem to about 1.2m (4ft) high.
		   Renovate sumach by cutting it back to almost ground level. This will result in numerous new shoots, which will subsequently need thinning out.

Ribes (flowering currant)	Deciduous shrub	*Flowers on the previous year's growth. Plants should be pruned annually after flowering to keep them vigorous and free flowering. Remove one in three or four stems, starting with the oldest.*
Robinia (false acacia)	Deciduous tree	*Prune in summer. It is important to maintain the main leader for as long as possible into the tree's early life, so all competing leaders must be removed as early as possible. Ensure that all main sideshoots are evenly and well spaced, and remove upright growth that appears close to the main trunk. Pruning of established trees is best kept to a minimum, but damaged and small, unwanted branches can be removed. Large cuts are prone to rotting.*
Rosa (rose)	Semievergreen/ deciduous shrub /climber	*See full pruning details on p112.*
Rosmarinus officinalis (rosemary)	Evergreen shrub	*Flowers on the previous year's growth. Established plants need little or no pruning, except to remove wayward and overlong shoots in early summer after flowering. Cut out any winter die-back in late spring. Plants can also be reshaped at this time, if needed. Old plants rarely reshoot well from old wood.*
Rubus (ornamental bramble)	Deciduous shrub	*Those grown for their stems should have the flowered growth removed to ground level in summer after flowering.* *Those grown for their flowers are pruned less severely, with just one in three or four of the oldest stems being cut back to ground level after flowering. Shorten the remaining stems by about one third to a vigorous shoot, to help maintain the shape.*

Plant name	Plant type	Pruning method
Salix (willow)	Deciduous shrub/tree	*Several shrubby willows are grown for their catkins and colourful winter stems. Prune these in spring, after the catkins have faded. Those grown for their winter stems should be pruned annually (see full pruning details on p44).* *Other shrubby willows need lighter, less regular pruning, although established plants can become woody and congested if left unpruned. Therefore, prune every other year, removing one in three stems, starting with the oldest.* *Willow trees can be pruned from autumn to early spring. The weeping 'Kilmarnock' willow (S. caprea 'Kilmarnock') is a small tree that forms an umbrella-shaped canopy of stiffly weeping branches. Although it needs little formative pruning, apart from removing unwanted stems, it does need annual pruning after a few years to prevent the crown from becoming congested. This should be done as the catkins fade. Remove around half of the oldest stems from the middle of the crown and any wayward ones growing in the wrong direction or increasing the width of the plant unnecessarily.*
Salvia (sage)	Evergreen shrub	*During the first spring after planting, tip back stems of S. officinalis to encourage bushy growth. Established plants can be kept compact and vigorous by cutting back during midspring. This will produce the best foliage displays from varieties grown for their ornamental foliage. Flowers are best removed in summer, by cutting back to strong growth. Old and neglected plants can be partially renovated by cutting back into old wood, but do not prune too hard.* *Pruning of the less hardy species is best kept to a minimum – remove any growth that has been killed by winter weather. Tip pruning of the branches in spring when growth starts will encourage bushy growth, and established plants can be cut back to a woody framework if necessary.*

185

Keep the pruning of established ornamental cherry (Prunus) trees to a minimum and, if needed, carry it out in summer.

Prune flowering currant (Ribes) immediately after flowering by removing some of the oldest stems.

Rosemary needs little or no regular pruning, and old plants rarely reshoot from old wood, so never hard prune these bushes.

Plant name	Plant type	Pruning method
Sambucus (elder)	Deciduous shrub	*Prune in winter when the plants are dormant. Remove old and weak shoots and open up the centre of congested plants; also trim back young shoots. In the second year, cut back two-year-old stems to just above ground level and one-year-old shoots by about one half.* *Those grown for their ornamental foliage are pruned hard annually, cutting back to ground level or to a low framework of branches. If you want to retain the height, shorten some stems in this way and then cut back the sideshoots on all remaining stems to two or three buds.*
Santolina (cotton lavender)	Evergreen shrub	*Needs regular pruning, otherwise it can become straggly and bare at the base. After planting, shorten stems by up to one third to encourage bushy growth. Thereafter, trim off faded flowers and wayward and overlong shoots annually, after flowering. If plants become straggly, hard prune in spring cutting back most of the previous year's growth.*
Sarcococca (winter box, Christmas box)	Evergreen shrub	*Winter box is grown for its shiny, evergreen foliage and highly scented, winter flowers produced on the previous year's growth. Little is needed in the way of regular pruning. Plants can be trimmed back and overlong and wayward stems removed, if necessary, in spring after flowering.*
Skimmia	Evergreen shrub	*This naturally dense, compact shrub needs little or no regular pruning. Lopsided growth and wayward stems can be shortened after flowering, cutting back to well within the bush to hide the cut shoots.*
Solanum (potato vine)	Semievergreen wall shrub	*After planting, remove the growing tips to promote bushy growth. Select 4–5 shoots to form the main framework and tie them to support wires. Prune established plants in spring (after any cold or frosty weather) by thinning out overcrowded growth and restricting size. Shorten shoots not needed to extend the framework back to 2–3 buds of their base.*
Sorbaria (false spiraea)	Deciduous shrub	*Prune in winter, completely removing one or two of the oldest stems and cutting back hard the previous year's flowered shoots.*
Sorbus (mountain ash, rowan, whitebeam)	Deciduous tree	*Generally needs little in the way of pruning, but any that is required should be carried out from autumn to early spring; dead wood can be removed in summer. After planting, formative prune to develop a single leader with five or six evenly and well-spaced sideshoots. Once established, there is little else that needs to be done other than the removal of damaged and crossing branches.*

Plant name	Plant type	Pruning method
Spartium (Spanish broom)	Deciduous shrub	*Flowers in summer and autumn on the current year's growth. Encourage new plants to produce a bushy habit by cutting back all new growth by about half during the first two springs after planting. Prune established shrubs every couple of years in spring, when growth starts, by cutting back the previous year's growth to within 5cm (2in) of older wood. If left unpruned, Spanish broom becomes topheavy and flowering is reduced.*
Spiraea	Deciduous shrub	*The spring flowers are produced on the previous year's stems or the summer ones on the current year's growth.* *Prune spring-flowering species after flowering. Cut back the flowered stems of young plants to strong buds, where new growth is emerging. Once established, cut back one in three or four of the oldest stems to ground level and shorten the remaining flowered shoots by up to one half.* *The summer-flowering species are pruned in late winter or early spring. Cut them back to a stubby framework of shoots 10–15cm (4–6in) above ground level – or even harder, to 5–7.5cm (2–3in) above ground level.*
Stachyurus	Deciduous shrub	*Needs little in the way of regular pruning, but old and thin growth can be cut down to its base, and overlong and wayward stems shortened by up to one third, in spring after flowering.*
Stephanandra	Deciduous shrub	*Thin plants in summer after flowering by removing one in three or four of the oldest stems to their base. Some of the remaining flowered stems should also be cut back to strong sideshoots.*
Symphoricarpos (snowberry)	Deciduous shrub	*Encourage new plants to produce thick, bushy growth by cutting back to 30cm (12in) after planting. In subsequent years, little or no pruning is necessary other than the removal of any misplaced or old twiggy growth in spring, to maintain a permanent framework. If snowberry spreads too far, restrict its growth by chopping away the excess suckers with a spade.*
Syringa (lilac)	Deciduous shrub	*Lilac is usually grown as a shrub, but common lilac (S. vulgaris) can also become tree-like with age. It flowers in spring and summer on the previous year's growth.* *Formative prune young plants in summer as the flowers fade, to encourage a well-balanced, bushy shape. Once established, carefully deadhead after flowering, if possible; take care not to damage the young shoots, which will carry the following year's flowers. At the same time, thin out weak and spindly shoots and, if space is tight, trim back some of the other stems.* *The more bushy lilacs, such as S. meyeri and S. pubescens subsp.* microphylla *'Superba', need minimal pruning, but can be cut back and thinned out if necessary after flowering.*

Plant name	Plant type	Pruning method
Tamarix (tamarisk)	Deciduous/evergreen shrub	*After planting, cut back all stems by one half to encourage a bushy habit; in the following year, similar pruning may be needed with plants that still look straggly.* *Species such as* T. parviflora *and* T. tentandra *flower in spring and early summer on the previous year's growth and are pruned in summer after flowering.* T. ramosissima *(syn.* T. pentandra*) flowers in late summer on the current year's growth and is pruned in early spring. Pruning consists of cutting back flowered growth to strong sideshoots. Late summer-flowering species can also be hard pruned to encourage more flowering and to keep the plants bushy.*
Thymus (thyme)	Evergreen shrub	*Regular pruning or shearing over after flowering will help keep plants neat and tidy, and ensure a steady supply of fresh leaves for use in cooking. Old thyme plants will not reshoot from old, woody growth.*
Tilia (lime, linden)	Deciduous tree	*Prune from midsummer to early winter; lime will bleed if pruned in spring. Train as a central-leader standard (see p60), ensuring there are even and well-spaced sideshoots to produce a balance crown.*
Trachelospermum (star jasmine, Confederate jasmine)	Evergreen climber	*Tie in young growth to the support wires – star jasmine needs no other formative pruning. In early spring, remove weak shoots and thin out overcrowded, congested growth. Tie in or remove any outward-growing shoots, and tip back overlong shoots to just above a flowering spur.*
Ulmus (elm)	Deciduous tree	*Prune from autumn to early spring. Most elms are grown as central-leader standards (see p60), although* U. parvifolia *and* U. pumila *are best left to grow without training and pruning. When a growing standard, ensure sideshoots are even and well spaced, removing any that are not; also tip prune any stems that compete with the leader. Established trees need little, if any pruning.*

Plant name	Plant type	Pruning method
Viburnum	Evergreen/deciduous shrub	*Only rarely needs regular annual pruning.* *Autumn- and winter-flowering* V. × bodnantense *and* V. farreri *produce their flowers on growth produced the previous summer. Established bushes produce new stems from the base and can have one in four or five of the oldest, weakest and most unproductive stems removed after flowering in early spring.* V. betulifolium, V. lantana, V. opulus *and* V. rhytidophyllum *are treated in the same way, but are best pruned in late winter.* V. tinus *has a long flowering period – from autumn through to spring – and should be pruned in spring or early summer after flowering. When young, it may need some formative pruning, but once established prune only to maintain the overall shape and height of the plant.* V. plicatum *flowers in late spring and early summer on the previous year's growth. Prune established plants in summer after flowering, removing old and unproductive growth and anything that spoils the overall shape of the plant.* V. × burkwoodii, V. × carlcephalum *and* V. carlesii *need minimum pruning, but if required this should be carried out in summer. The groundcover* V. davidii *needs only wayward shoots removing, which will also help to keep it compact.*
Vinca (periwinkle)	Evergreen shrub	*To prevent periwinkle from becoming invasive, remove any unwanted shoots in spring. You can even use shears or a nylon-line trimmer to cut back large areas of ground cover.*
Vitis (ornamental vine)	Deciduous climber	*Always carry out any major pruning in winter before the sap begins to rise, otherwise plants may bleed to death.* *After planting, pinch out the growing tips and select two or three shoots to form the main framework. Once the framework is established, shorten all the previous year's growth to 2–3 buds on the main branches. Tip back excessive growth to a bud in summer.* *For grapevines, see full pruning details on p160.*
Weigela	Deciduous shrub	*Flowers on the previous year's growth. Prune plants annually after flowering, to encourage strong, new growth for the following year's display. Cut back flowered stems to strong shoots below the flowers. At the same time, if the plant is large enough, cut down 1–2 old stems to their base, then shorten overlong and wayward growth.*
Wisteria	Deciduous climber	*See full pruning details on p90.*

• INDEX •

190

191

• PICTURE CREDITS •

Note The acknowledgements below appear in source order.

....

Alamy John Glover 45, 134; Rex Argent 82

Fotolia beerfan 150; Colette 131; daseaford 138; Felinda 56; Foto sapiens 126; Horticulture 10, 19 above, 98, 149; Jean-Jacques Cordier 36; John Photon 162; Monika Rojewska 152; qualitatsgrafik 144; Robert Scoverski 28; Tetiana Zbrodko 132

GAP Photos BBC Magazines Ltd 18, 69; BIOS/Gilles Le Scanff & Joëlle-Caroline Mayer 21; Clive Nichols 72 below; Elke Borkowski 12, 53, 84, 95; FhF Greenmedia 72 above; Friedrich Strauss 7, 42; J S Sira 65; Jerry Harpur 125; Juliette Wade 155; Lee Avison 109; Michael Howes 6; Neil Holmes 143; Richard Bloom 19 below; Rob Whitworth 141; S & O Mathews 107; Sarah Cuttle 2; Tim Gainey 59; Zara Napier 16, 103

Garden Collection Derek Harris 41; Liz Eddison/design: Haruko Seki and Makoto Saito, RHS Chelsea 2008 47; Neil Sutherland 86

Garden World Images Dave Bevan 81; John Martin 181 left; Lynne Mack 110; Martin Hughes-Jones 175 left; Mein Schöner Garten 15; Rex Richardson 113; Rowan Isaac 35; Geoff Hodge 17 left and right

Octopus Publishing Group Torie Chugg 159

Photolibrary Buro Kloeg/Niels Kooijman 76; Garden Picture Library/Mark Bolton 79; Garden Picture Library/Mark Winwood 75; Garden Picture Library/Michael Howes 31

Thinkstock Hemera 91, 93, 175 right, 181 centre, 185 left and centre; iStockphoto 9, 49, 114, 116, 123, 169 all, 175 centre, 181 right, 185 right; Valueline 11